D0055698

Jordan, David L.,
David L. Jordan :
36095002856571
MMRLS-WAL

David L. Jordan

92
Jordan
Mississ

3-22-16

25⁰⁰

David L. Jordan

From the Mississippi Cotton Fields
to the State Senate, A Memoir

David L. Jordan with Robert L. Jenkins

Foreword by Mike Espy

University Press of Mississippi   Jackson

Mid-Mississippi Regional Library System
Attala, Holmes, Leake, Montgomery
and Winston Counties

Willie Morris Books in Memoir and Biography

www.upress.state.ms.us

The University Press of Mississippi is a member
of the Association of American University Presses.

Photographs are from the author's collection unless otherwise noted.

Copyright © 2014 by David L. Jordan
All rights reserved
Manufactured in the United States of America

First printing 2014
∞
Library of Congress Cataloging-in-Publication Data
Jordan, David L., 1933–
  David L. Jordan : from the Mississippi cotton fields to the state senate / David L.
Jordan with Robert L. Jenkins.
    pages cm. — (Willie Morris books in memoir and biography)
  Includes index.
  ISBN 978-1-61703-966-9 (cloth : alk. paper) — ISBN 978-1-61703-967-6 (ebook) 1.
Jordan, David L., 1933– 2. African American politicians—Mississippi—Biography.
3. Civil rights workers—Mississippi—Biography. 4. Civil rights movements—Mis-
sissippi—History—20th century. 5. Political participation—Mississippi—History—
20th century. 6. African Americans—Mississippi—Politics and government—20th
century. 7. Mississippi—Race relations—Political aspects—History—20th century.
8. Racism--Mississippi—History—20th century. 9. Till, Emmett, 1941–1955. 10.
Trials (Murder)—Mississippi—Sumner. I. Jenkins, Robert L., 1945– II. Title.
  E185.97.J775A3 2014
  302.092—dc23
  [B]   2013028817

British Library Cataloging-in-Publication Data available

To my great-grandchildren,
Zeliah, Briana, Caleigh, and Ashlyn

Contents

Foreword

Despite the thickness of the evening air, the dutiful men and women of the Greenwood Voters' League fanned themselves more slowly, in deferential anticipation of their president, who was next to speak. As his tall and angular frame took hold of the microphone, the membership understood that standing before them was a man of substance and consequence—their significant leader, whose stirring oratory could unleash popular reaction across the Mississippi Delta.

This was David Jordan, a name revered in the black community, and a name respected, albeit grudgingly, in the white community. A nod from David Jordan could ensure an election, incite a boycott, or inspire a young man such as myself to aspire one day to hold a seat in the U.S. Congress.

I was there on that sweltering August evening, attending my first meeting of the Greenwood Voters' League, and observed one who, not unlike Nelson Mandela, easily wears the mantle of leadership, because the community he serves extended to him their absolute confidence and unconditional respect. It is an unspoken, reciprocal kind of respect that can project and challenge a community toward unknown heights.

Perhaps not as well known nationally as Medgar Evers, or Fannie Lou Hamer, David Jordan stands as every bit a peerless icon—another essential driver, as such, on freedom's road. It's a good thing that he has written an autobiography so some will learn and others will not forget what the enthralled members of the Greenwood Voters' League have understood for decades: that David Jordan is a social "champion," and a veritable force not to be underestimated.

Because of his personal sacrifice during some very menacing times, and moreover because of his victories that advanced multiple political and civil rights causes, David Jordan has more than earned the title "a man of the people." He offers an insightful book that demonstrates why he is still so highly regarded for his wisdom, courage, and instincts for social activism.

From the Mississippi Cotton Fields to the State Senate chronicles Senator Jordan's rise from humble beginnings in the Jim Crow South to influential office in the state capitol, serving as the senator representing a still impoverished people. Through stories and anecdotes, he provides a glimpse of the harsh socioeconomic conditions imposed upon the agricultural laborers of the region, which forged within him the desire to seek justice at whatever cost and through whatever means necessary.

His book gives us personal insight into the Emmett Till murder and provides witness to other seminal events such as the Freedom Rides, which fundamentally changed our nation.

As architect of civil disobedience campaigns, as named plaintiff in lawsuits demanding educational and political equity, and through successive wins at the ballot box, David Jordan has pushed back against the boundaries artificially placed to retard black achievement in the South. He has achieved high office personally, and through his efforts, he has led the way for numerous others who had once only dared to stand for political office in the post-Reconstruction era.

His literary work shall, in libraries, on home bookshelves, and within digital e-readers across the nation, be read by students and others who desire greater background on the great civil rights movement, and who long for greater insight regarding strategic decisions made during those dangerous times.

David Jordan has advised presidents and governors and I know has provided valuable guidance and counsel to me in all of my political endeavors. But no matter how high he rises, at his core he will always be the president of the Voters' League. And the members will always be grateful for that fact.

Mike Espy
Former U.S. Secretary of Agriculture during President Clinton's Administration

Acknowledgments

There are many people who are responsible for helping me, as I am a first-time writer. It took their love, patience, encouragement, and understanding in order to make this journey "from the Mississippi cotton fields to the state senate."

I thank my wife, Christine, for her patience and understanding about the long hours I spent writing this book; my children, David Jr., Joyce and Larry, Donald, Darryl and Jennifer, for their support and encouragement for me to continue; my grandchildren, Larry Jr., Stephanie and Chad, Loren, Heir, Hope Lindsey, Sela, and Robin; and my great-grandchildren, Zeliah, Briana, Caleigh, and Ashlyn, for encouraging their papa to write this book.

Many thanks to the outstanding people in my life like Mike Espy, the first African American to become U.S. Secretary of Agriculture, for writing the foreword to this book, and to the vice president of the Greenwood Voters' League, Robert Sims, for his patience and for sticking by me. Special thanks go to Mrs. Eloise Gray, treasurer of the Greenwood Voters' League, for giving me the title of this book and to my sister, Mrs. Viola Sisson, for adding to my recollections of the family's history.

I appreciate the *Greenwood Commonwealth* newspaper for the many articles concerning me as president of the Greenwood Voters' League, as a member of the Greenwood City Council, and as a state senator. Thanks to the media, especially WABG-TV and WXVT-TV, for information relating to their coverage of press conferences and other stories of importance in telling my story. Thanks to the Indianola public schools, the schools of Humphrey, Carroll, and Holmes counties, and the Greenwood school district for the tenure of thirty-three years of teaching science. Regarding the legal community, thanks to attorney James Littleton and attorney Willie J. Perkins for their friendship and support. Finally, to Dr. Robert Jenkins, retired history professor, who knew of my interest in writing this book from its inception and whose advice and encouragement along the way helped moved the project forward: thanks for your support and your work in helping to bring this book to fruition.

David L. Jordan

Prologue

There is no place in the world that can represent the South better than the Mississippi Delta. This is the very place where the scorching sun beamed on the brows of blacks slaving on antebellum and postbellum plantations, the place where black people were deprived of a decent education and exposed to limited opportunities. The controversial issues of racism that have ruled the state of Mississippi for decades still have many wondering if equality will ever truly exist in the place that sparked, arguably, the modern civil rights movement. The brutal deaths of Emmett Till and Medgar Evers triggered a burning desire for justice. The unleashing of the vicious dogs on African Americans to keep them from registering to vote also left a bitter taste in the mouths of black Americans. These incidents that I speak about happened in Greenwood, Leflore County, or are certainly identified with this area. I can still visualize the face of Medgar Evers's killer who frequently visited the store where I was employed as a young man. The attacks on African Americans with dogs also started in Greenwood. These heinous acts of brutality were enough to ignite a fire in blacks who shaped the civil rights movement, particularly as it evolved in Mississippi. There are certain visions that I wish I could erase from my memory, but I have come to understand that these images are all part of my history, that I must confront this history and not escape from it.

I often wonder if racial hatred will ever be removed from some people's hearts. In the summer of 2006, Emmett Till's highway marker was covered in red letters that read "KKK," not far away from the same river where his distorted body had floated fifty years previously. There are many who would like to believe that such things are simply isolated events and unfairly still label Mississippi with an ugly stigma. They unabashedly say that the days of inequality are far behind us, even in the Mississippi Delta. But is that really the case? I think not. Blatant injustices involving African Americans continue to make the headlines. They have validated awareness that the struggle for justice continues. This struggle includes the controversy regarding the state flag, a flag featuring the Confederate symbol that still flies over the state grounds. The controversial symbol showed by popular vote that it evokes truly divisive emotions when 65 percent of Mississippians viewed it as representative of a proud history, but 35 percent of the citizenry regarded it a relic of Jim Crow oppression. The decision to keep the flag was stunning, and left me wondering! Here stood a golden opportunity to put the past where it belonged; we obviously failed to see the significance of embracing new beginnings. The continuing struggle for justice could also be the denigrating practice of segregation that periodically crept boldly into the school districts. The practice was ordered by the court to desist more than forty years ago but reappears in new ways far too often. A Mississippi middle school in August of 2010 was brought to the forefront because of its racial policy in electing the president of the student council. Sixth-to-eighth graders were told that in order to seek the position of council president the candidate had to be white. This is a school where 72 percent of the four hundred students are white, but it sent a clear and degrading message to the whole student body, especially to the other 28 percent. Then there is my old school buddy Morgan Freeman, whose campaign to integrate a high school prom in Mississippi took eleven long years. In 1997 Morgan Freeman challenged the existence of a racial divide on a day that should be remembered as a happy and memorable occasion for high schoolers. He promised to pay all senior prom expenses if the affair was racially integrated. It was not until 2008 that Freeman saw his kind and generous gesture of unity become a reality.

Another shocking event that certainly stirred a painful memory in me occurred when a black man was found hanging from a tree in North Greenwood in December of 2010. The local authorities ruled the death an apparent suicide, but questions surrounding the case certainly leave room for doubt. When I visited the crime scene, the sadness that quickly came over me was like reliving a terrible nightmare. Whether such a violent death was self-inflicted or caused by some other force, the result was way too familiar, reminiscent of an earlier period of my life. These are just a few incidents that make me aware that the existence of racial discrimination is still in today's society.

I have been in the trenches of many battles during my sixty-year journey for justice and in this time I have seen the display of many forms of racism. There are some who question the real motives attached to the voice of David Jordan. They wonder who I am and ask why I love black people so much, but I have seen with my very own eyes the terrible things that African Americans have endured simply because of who we are. I look at where my people are, where I come from and where I am, and the realities keep me focused on what it is that I am supposed to be doing. I made a decision a long time ago that I wouldn't ignore issues that we as African Americans should be concerned about. Some have gone as far as to call me a racist because of the positions I take, but a racist is not who I am and I have no hatred in my heart for anyone. It doesn't mean that because I have a strong compassion for my own people that I dislike white people. I feel only pity for people who discriminate against a person because of race, color, or creed. Clearly there comes a time when we must face the differences that make the world a unique place, but accepting differences should not create a climate that leads to stereotyping and misrepresentation. If we can't be concerned about what is happening to our own people then what are we really about? What do we stand for and what really matters at the end of the day? The thought of knowing that I've tried to make a wrong turn right creates a feeling in me beyond description and this feeling makes the journey I've endured, however tumultuous it has often been, worth traveling.

I can remember the uncontrollable tears flowing from my wife's eyes and mine once we received the dreadful news that Dr. Martin Luther King Jr. had been assassinated. It was like losing a family member, knowing that a man who was wholly dedicated to the welfare of our people died at the hands of a racist filled with violent hatred. It's been these types of inexcusable acts that have left blacks feeling hopeless and quite fearful that racial justice will never prevail and create an equal playing field for blacks and whites. It's like an automatic reaction that overwhelms me when it becomes necessary to fight for the things that I truly believe in. That is why *Jordan v. Greenwood,* which was a chance to change the form of city government in Greenwood, Mississippi, was a lawsuit that I didn't think twice about pursuing in 1977. I sued the city simply because I wanted to see blacks have an opportunity to be represented in local government. It eventually led to my becoming the president of the first black majority city council in Greenwood's history. It also served notice that David Jordan would confront issues where unfair policies were common practice. There are no issues of injustice that I will not assault and no unlawful deeds that I will not challenge. As one popular writer once penned it, I have seen the worst and the best of times. The memories that I have collected over the years have certainly brought me a sense of gratification and a deep appreciation for the struggles and lessons I encountered along the way of my personal life journey. To be the son of a Mississippi sharecropper and find a way to serve and lead my people affords a deep sense of fulfillment.

The faces of courageous people who have crossed my path have been remarkable as well as unforgettable. Whether living or now dead, they were often people of great stature and they left such an everlasting mark on our racial and national history. I remember engaging in a conversation with Rosa Parks and hearing from her own mouth that the death of Emmett Till is what triggered her refusal to give up her bus seat to a white man. It sent a chill down my spine to be engaged in a conversation with someone so resolute, whose strong belief in a cause made her a national heroine. I'm sure Rosa Parks had no idea that she was making history by fighting against something that she felt was unfair. It was also a badge of honor to arrange for a place in Greenwood where Dr. King could speak. Of course, that turned into a difficult task because there were many blacks terrified of the possible consequences of associating with such a powerful man. I was finally able to secure a place that was honored to host the great Dr. King. A minister by the name of Rev. William Wallace, rest his soul, had the guts to open up his small church for the event and it turned into a glorious occasion. I will never forget that date of March 16, 1968, when Dr. King visited Greenwood and how he spoke with such an abundance of faith and confidence. He was truly a man who wasn't fearful, which made his enemies even more concerned about his influence; but tragically a few weeks later he was cowardly gunned down in Memphis, Tennessee.

There is no situation too big or small where racism might be the root of the problem that should be overlooked, and I have learned the importance of always acting with a sense of urgency. We must never get comfortable enough to accept mediocre treatment tinged with an undertone of racial prejudice; those days are, and should be, far behind us. I have seen great leaders gone way too soon, so it's up to the ones left behind to ensure that no premature death ever goes in vain. It may appear to some that the frequent painful realities of my journey cause me to overlook the progress that has been made. I will be the first to admit that we have come a long way, but I know that there is still work ahead of us. I know that we are headed in the right direction, despite the obstacles occasionally thrown in our path. I experienced firsthand a milestone in my political career, so I know that changes are helping us move forward.

It was the 2004 Democratic National Convention in Boston that stands out in my mind. My wife, Chris, usually accompanied me to these events, but at this particular one I was alone. An African American male made his way to the podium and began speaking. It wasn't long before I was inquiring about him—who he was and where he had come from. It was something about the well-expressed words he used that immediately made me identify with a man filled with his confidence and hope, but most of all his patience and understanding. It was a dynamic speech that earned him a standing ovation from the diverse crowd. I remember on the flight home, one of my colleagues asked me what I thought about this man who obviously had made such a great impression on so many people in attendance. I simply stated that I felt this man was going places, but I didn't know he would go on to make history and create such a defining moment in the life of this nation in general, and mine in particular. There are no words to describe the feeling inside of me when, as a presidential elector, I cast the vote for the state of Mississippi for the first black Democratic Party nominee for president of the United States. It was indeed the highlight of my political career to see President Barack Obama become the forty-fourth president of the United States in January 2009. I couldn't help but think of Poppa because he always wanted one of his children to meet the president. I'm sure he turned over in his grave to know that I cast the vote for the first black president and that was definitely history in the making. On November 6, 2012, President Obama was reelected for a second term.

As I look back over my journey, I chuckle to myself because I have come a long way from hanging my head low and simply saying, "Yes, sir!" to white people. The dedication and commitment toward something that comes so natural to me now is definitely worth any pain and suffering that I have endured over the years. I believe there are some people who don't like David Jordan for one reason or another, but at bottom, that is because they don't understand me. It's so much easier to criticize from the back seat than to be courageous enough to allow one's voice to be heard from the front seat. I didn't get involved in the fight for justice for personal gain, and whatever respect I receive I have tried to earn. I want coming generations to continue to look to a future of, as Dr. King said, being judged by the content of their character and not by the color of their skin. This is one battle that I will continue to fight until they mark my grave. I hope that after reading this book many people will see that David Jordan isn't a bad man. I'm simply a man who refuses to allow ignorance, prejudice, and hatred to write my epitaph!

Born into
the Cotton Field

I was born April 3, 1933, in a world quite different from the one we know today. I was born during a difficult era, in a decade known as the Great Depression. It was a period when the world saw the longest and deepest depression experienced by the industrialized world. It was clearly a miserable time, a period when nearly half of the children didn't have adequate food, shelter, or even medical care. In the year of my birth, national unemployment had reached its worse point. However, all was not gloom and doom; certainly some positive things occurred. For example, there were national historical landmarks built, which included the Empire State Building, the Chrysler Building, the Golden Gate Bridge, and Rockefeller Center. Franklin Roosevelt's New Deal legislation provided far-reaching social and economic reforms that continue to affect positively American life to this day. Yet, the Great Depression will remain the best example of how far the world's economic status can actually decline and rebound. It will also always mark the time when great leaders who had a significant impact on our history were born!

My parents, Elizabeth and Cleveland Jordan, saw their fifth child born during those hard and treacherous times on the Lawyer Whittington Plantation, approximately two miles north of Greenwood, in Leflore County, Mississippi. The plantations of the period were named after the owners and Mr. Whittington was the owner of this place. My parents named me David Lee Jordan. I was the fourth boy born into the Jordan clan. When I think back, it becomes crystal clear to me that my parents were a shining example of what strong family ties represent. The idea of sticking together as a family through hard times and painful disappointments established a strong bond not often apparent in a lot of black families in today's society.

My parents were instrumental in my developing at an early age a strong desire to stand up for something I truly believed in. My mother, Elizabeth Jordan, was an attractive woman with a smile so stunning that it gave me comfort each time it spread across her face. Momma was a strong, quiet woman, standing a little over five feet, with black wavy hair and a smooth copper skin tone that could easily have had her mistaken for being of Native American blood. It wasn't until she opened her mouth and a southern melodic voice emerged that one could be sure of her African American heritage. Momma was a lady of few words, but her dedication to her husband and children was definitely always loud and clear. Never in her lifetime did she make enough money to equal her worth, but it didn't stop her from being good at what she did. She was an excellent worker as well as a fantastic cook; even to this day I still haven't tasted fried chicken better than hers. My father, Cleveland Jordan, was a man of average height whose stern disposition was something not to be taken lightly. His dark complexion and the gold teeth in his mouth didn't keep him from being a handsome man in my eyes. My daddy's quick temper, stern persona, and sturdy hand didn't keep him from earning the name "Poppa." He would whack you with anything that he could get his hands on when his temper got the best of him, but his anger never made us doubt his love for the family. He was also a religious man who strongly believed in God, but sometimes he could not control the cuss words that flowed from his mouth when his anger button was sufficiently pushed. It took a while before I realized it, but I finally came to understand that my father was just a proud black man who truly cared about his people.

Poppa always took the time to share stories with us of the troubled things he had witnessed and that had such a huge impact on his life. I remember just like it was yesterday a particular story he shared with us. Poppa spoke of a time that he and three men of color decided to challenge the procedure in place for using their coupon book. This book was used as payment for groceries bought every two weeks with the money earned picking cotton. Poppa decided that he wanted cash money instead of the coupon booklet, so he encouraged the three men to join him in asking the "boss man" for cash. Of course, Poppa told us, when it was time to confront the boss with the request he was standing alone. He said that he never forgot the look on Mr. Whittington's face when he confronted him on that Saturday morning. Mr. Whittington said to my poppa, "Cleveland, if you weren't such a good nigga, I would kill you! Those other niggas came here and got their groceries last night, and told me of your plot! So, you know the only thing that is saving you is that you're a good working nigga!"

My poppa, with his head hanging low, simply said, "Yes, sir!" He got his groceries with the coupon book. His sack weighed heavy on his shoulder as he headed in the direction of home. I later realized the point of Poppa's story was for us to learn early that we might be forced to stand alone for something that we believed in. That was just one of the many lessons that Poppa taught us in his own special way. Understandably, we were taught early to stay in our place when it came to interacting with white folks. It simply meant to get out of their way, speak only when spoken to, and to run like hell in the direction of home if it appeared that trouble was on the horizon. It reminded me of the Saturday afternoons when all the kids went to the pecan grove to pick pecans. Momma would always hand me a small pillowcase to hold the pecans that I picked. She would then look at me with emotion visible in her eyes and softly say, "Remember, Momma and Poppa love you." I knew that was her reassurance, just in case something happened while we were away that kept us from returning home. It was just that type of world and you never knew when being the wrong color could cost you a scolding, a beating, or even your life.

My parents definitely did everything in their power to protect me and my siblings. The oldest brother, Clevester, was the one in the family who kept my parents the most worried until he went off to World War II. Clevester spent the time he wasn't working in the field getting into trouble. He dropped out of school and ran around with a group of boys that fought and kept up problems on the plantation. Momma's nerves stayed on edge worrying about him, especially after he was stabbed in the back of the neck participating in what is known today as gang activity. My brother did have one skill that he mastered and that was riding the mule. He quickly earned himself the nickname of "Zetty." It was so fascinating for me to watch Clevester's shirt tail flapping in the wind from the speed of the mule. It brought even more of a smile on my face to know that he was my big brother. By the time my brother and I started developing a relationship, he was forced to go off to the war. We all hated to say goodbye to him because deep down inside we had no idea if we would ever see his face again. Momma worried from the time that Clevester was drafted into the military and even afterwards when he was discharged and went north to start a new life.

My brother Will Henry was next in line, and probably the only one of my siblings who was a little more withdrawn than the rest of us. Will was a child who stayed to himself, and I can't begin to count the times that he got his behind whipped. He refused to communicate in school and even Poppa's switch wasn't enough to make him speak up. Will realized at an early age that school was something he just wasn't interested in. His attention span was never focused on learning so he eventually dropped out before he even completed grade school. Will was the brother that I could always count on to be my shield of protection because he definitely had a mean streak. He reacted to almost everything that he didn't appreciate, and something as simple as staring at him too long could trigger a reaction. I often worried about him because I never knew if his anger and frustration would be detrimental to him if he ran into the wrong person.

My sister, Viola, was the only girl born into the Jordan family and she was also the middle child. As the only girl, Viola quickly acquired the nickname "Sister," a name that identifies her to this day. Being the only girl also meant she was placed in charge of us boys to a certain degree. She was like a second mother to us when it came to distributing our school lunches that Momma packed for us daily. She also made sure we didn't get involved in too much mischievous behavior. Sister, however, was like one of the boys when it came to work and play. She was what one could call a "tomboy." It didn't matter that Sister wore a dress because she was like one of us when it came to climbing trees and swimming in the creek. I knew deep down inside that Viola had to enjoy being the only girl at times because it kept her from having to share her sleeping quarters. It also gave her some private time to herself. She had her own bed across from us in the small bedroom that all the kids shared in our two-room bungalow home. Our living arrangements didn't really matter that much anyway because it seemed as if we spent more time in the field than we did in our own house.

My parents were really committed to Sister receiving her education. They wanted all of us to learn, but there were special provisions made for Sister that allowed her to stay on course when it came to her education. She picked cotton in the field from August until October. After that time period ended she was sent to live with a lady by the name of Miss Hattie Sheppard. This occurred in order for Sister to attend public school in town. The family would even pick cotton at night, so that enough cotton was already picked when it was time for Sister to head off to school. Viola was a good sister and quite responsible for her age.

The next boy in the family and the closest to me in age was Andrew. He received his cotton picking sack by the age of three and he was also considered to be my overseer when I was a baby. It was Andrew who had the responsibility of making sure Momma knew when I cried due to hunger pains. I was nursed in the cotton field up to the age of two or three. It was the way things were back then. Mothers breast-fed their children until they were toddler age. When I give it some thought, I suspect that breast-feeding was probably one of the reasons that children did not get so sick from simple maladies. Of course, many home remedies also helped. There was no such thing back then as today's immunization shots. We depended on the good health of our mothers to provide us with the nourishment and nutrients that a young body needs. Andrew was also the closest one to my dreams, as we shared a small space at the foot of the bed. Our two older brothers, Clevester and Will, slept at the head of the bed. Andrew and I did almost everything together, from household chores to fishing in the nearby creek. We even engaged in a rock throwing rivalry with the other boys on the plantation. There was one family in particular that we stayed into it with and that was the "Sandy Gizzard Boys." They lived in the wooded area in the back of the plantation and they would have to pass our house en route to the store to get supplies. We would then shower the five Sandy Gizzard brothers with rocks and dirt clogs as they passed by. It was mischievous behavior of this nature that often kept Andrew and me snickering at night until we drifted off to sleep.

Everyone in the family except me was picking cotton, the sacks ranging in length according to the picker's size and strength. It was established early on that Andrew was the best cotton picker in the family. Laborers picked cotton that grew in long rows; we worked, like the slaves did in the antebellum period of the cotton culture, from sunrise to sunset. By the end of the cotton picking year, Poppa was asking the owner for the worn cotton sacks that were used throughout the year. To the owner of the plantation it was a reminder of my family's hard work, but to us those sacks were used as bed sheets to cover our bodies.

I only spent one year on the Lawyer Whittington Plantation before my father packed up the wagon and headed to our new home, which was the Charles Whittington Plantation. There was only a six-mile separation between the two plantations, but it turned into a long eight-hour journey. The two mules pulled the wagon that was covered with a canvas to shield us from the bitter cold rain. We traveled along gravel roads surrounded by woods in order to get to our new location. Our new bungalow home was small and not filled with the familiar comforts found in the modern homes of today. Indeed, it was entirely too small for a family of seven, but we made the best of it. There was no electrical power, so our source of light was the kerosene lamps. All of our plumbing needs were set up behind the house. The water used for bathing came from a well and we even had to use the bathroom outside. These were just a few examples of the inconveniences we were faced with, but there were many families in worse shape than we were.

I was two years old when I first got carried to the cotton field and soon after that I acquired my own cotton sack. It was now a family of seven, picking cotton throughout the long day. It wasn't long before my family was picking three bales of cotton a week, but certainly not from a lot of contribution from me. I was the weakest worker in the family when it came to picking cotton and it remained that way until the end of my cotton picking days. I stayed in trouble throughout the years because I was frequently caught daydreaming in the field. I knew at an early age that I didn't want to spend the rest of my life doing something that was so menial and which negatively affected my sense of self-worth. I wanted to use my brain for something much more than just standing on my feet all day with the sizzling sun beaming down on my head. We received eleven dollars per bale as a family, which came out to thirty-three dollars a week. The money was mainly used on groceries and this included the usual items that filled most black croppers' cabinets. Foods like pork and beans, oil sausage, salmon, and molasses were always part of our purchases. We also had a few foods that were planted and harvested in our small family garden, such as sweet potatoes and greens, which were treats that we didn't have too often. We had two cows, our source of fresh milk. It always seemed like our food supplies were barely enough, but somehow they proved sufficient to keep us going. At the end of the cotton picking year Poppa would take us to get one pair of shoes. Those shoes had to last throughout the year, even though they wore out quickly from the constant use. It was a big deal to have a pair of shoes back then because so many children missed school due to the embarrassment of not having anything to put on their feet. The reality of walking barefooted on the hot ground was simply too much for some to bear. I was extremely grateful that Poppa made sure that the cost of covering our feet was added to a very tight family budget.

It's certain that I remember more bad times than good ones on the plantation, but we did share some laughs and fun. It was true back then that black people had to establish their own type of fun and turn what appeared to be a dim situation into brightness. The normal joy that most children desire today was the same joy that my siblings and I looked forward to. I remember us anxiously flipping through the Sears catalog hoping that Christmas would show up at our doorstep. Taking turns running to let our parents know what things in the catalog had captured our attention was quite a thrill. Any joy during that time was something that we savored and held in our memory until the next happy occasion.

It was always a great feeling when I could block out the horror stories that I constantly heard involving people of color. These stories included how black men were being severely punished if they were caught even attempting to speak to a white woman. To be found interacting with a white woman was one of the black man's greatest fears. I learned at an early age to stay as far from trouble as I could, and perhaps being the youngest gave me a little extra protection. Moreover, my parents made it crystal clear that part of my siblings' responsibilities was to look after me.

The summertime represented the same thoughts of fun as it does today. There were certain outside activities that became more enjoyable around that time of year. I was around the age of five or six when I really began to look forward to the summertime. We picked berries and there was a June berry that was referred to as dewberry that Momma used to make dewberry pie. She would mix it with flour and then place a cover on top of it and serve it as Sunday's dessert. It was delicious, and it was certainly a treat to look forward to. The summer also was when we went to catch fish. We often used a popular method called "muddying" for fish. Andrew and I, along with two of our friends from the plantation, Jet T. Sutton and Melvin McCoy, would go and catch the fish that had been trapped in shallow waters during the winter months. We would make the fish come to the surface, capture them with a long three-prong fork, and then take them home. The most common fish around that time was the "bony fish," so called because it *was* filled with many bones. I can't count the times that either Momma or Poppa would have to turn me upside down just to get a bone out of my throat from eating bony fish. Momma usually sat next to me and did her best to pick all the bones out of my fish, but there were times that she couldn't be by my side holding my hand. There were simply going to be certain things that she just couldn't protect me from, although she wanted to.

The week of the Fourth of July holiday also brought a little excitement for "colored people." That was the time when the chicken fights came near the plantation. A man by the name of Joe Williams was in charge of the chicken fights. Fight handlers put steel spurs on the roosters' feet and let them attack each other. The white folks would gather around and bet on which rooster would kill the other one. After the fight they often would throw the dead roosters into the crowd of black folks who were anxiously hoping to take home a free meal. Andrew and I accompanied Poppa a couple of times and we actually got a kick out of watching the festivities. The fights lasted all week and Poppa didn't miss a day being there hoping to catch a bird. By Thursday night, at the end of the fight, the dead roosters would be prepared for the big barbecue. We would stay up past midnight hoping that Poppa would walk through the door with a bag of barbecue in his hand and in most cases he did; that way on the Fourth of July we could celebrate with a barbecue. It was great to have families gathered around having fun and inhaling the aroma of hickory-smoked barbecue. A black man by the name of Mr. Piggy would barbecue all the chickens for Mr. Williams and it was some of the best barbecue a person ever tasted.

The summer also served as a minivacation away from picking cotton. It was customary that all cotton was "laid by" on the first day of August because the fruit was on the way. This allowed us to have a two- or three-week rest period before we had to start picking cotton again. Everyone looked forward to that time, just to take a breather away from all the hard and continuous work, even if was only a brief rest.

I began to understand as I grew older how the system on the plantation actually worked. We were considered sharecroppers, and though the details sometimes differed, the sharecropping system was as follows. If the croppers picked thirty bales of cotton, then fifteen went to the plantation owner and fifteen to the sharecroppers. It was the sharecroppers' responsibility to pay the expenses of fertilizer, cultivation, seeds, and interest out of their fifteen bales. Needless to say, this wasn't a truly fair split. We received what the older generation referred to as a "draw-day," which meant in modern terms an allotment. We also gave half of the foods that we planted and harvested to the plantation owner. If we pulled ten loads of corn, then automatically half of the harvest belonged to the owner of the plantation, Mr. Whittington. There was always a set of eyes watching us to make sure that we were being fair when it came to distributing the corn. It didn't matter that it was our hard work that pulled the corn. We used a wagon to be sure that the corn got delivered to the barn, where Mr. Whittington would wait for his half. This was just the way things were and it didn't appear that anything was going to change anytime soon.

I continued to be by my family's side as we carried out our cotton picking duties. It was decided that since I couldn't pick much cotton I would be the one to haul the cotton to the gin. I would take the cotton to the gin in a wagon, position it to be sucked up through a pipe, and then wait for Mr. Luther Rucker, the gin operator, to give me a receipt. I was referred to as "little nigger Jordan" in reference to me being a member of the Jordan family. It was quite degrading to be referred to in that manner. The word "nigger" was so commonly used on the plantation, however, that it was pretty much a household name for all blacks. Mr. Hodges, the plantation bookkeeper, certainly referred to all the blacks on the plantation as "niggers." He was a much older white man, around eighty, and he was just set in his ways.

I would run back to the field once I received the money and place it in Poppa's hand. He would then turn it over to Momma because she was the one who managed the family budget. We would sometimes receive a nickel together, but there were times that my siblings and I got a nickel apiece. A nickel back then could purchase a lot of candy. We would be extremely excited to have treats that would last us most of the night. Our bedtime was 8:00 p.m. and there were no exceptions made. We could count on Poppa waking us up at 4:30 a.m. to head off to the cotton field. It was crystal clear that everything we enjoyed would definitely be earned and not just given.

I was coming of school age and I wanted to learn. I wanted to discover certain things that were not clear to me. But I truly wanted an opportunity to learn more about myself. I was ready to understand the value of receiving an education, something that in many instances today has been taken for granted. In the years of my youth the reality of formal learning and advancing was a struggle to achieve, not an opportunity. We stress education today to ensure that black children have every opportunity available to them. They have every tool necessary to compete in today's society, but unfortunately that wasn't my reality back then. It was understood that there was absolutely no way educating blacks would ever come before the hard work that was required to enrich only the white planters.

The Struggle
for an Education

My education began in 1940 at the tender age of seven in a church called Traveler's Rest. It was in the country right down the road from where we lived on the Whittington Plantation. There were no public schools for African Americans on the plantations back then so formal learning wasn't going to come easily. It was a racially discriminatory situation during those times, as only whites were allowed easy access to public schools where they could receive a decent education. There was a rule that children on the plantations couldn't start school until all the cotton was picked. The school year lasted from December to April. It was already difficult learning under the conditions that we were subjected to and a short school session made it that much harder.

By the 1940s a wealthy Jewish family had started to build schools in the South for African American children. These were the much needed and appreciated Rosenwald schools. In 1941 the fund built a school in Leflore County called the Ellis School, named after the principal, Professor L. S. Ellis. He was an older gentleman, who I believe received his degree from Alcorn State University. Professor Ellis was a man of average height with a heavy build, but his mean disposition made him as deadly as a rattlesnake. All the children knew that getting in trouble with him resulted in severe consequences. Professor Ellis would require all the students to line up every morning, the boys on one side and the girls on the other. He would slowly walk past the lineup with a bell in one hand and a switch in the other. It was like an army inspection because we had to stand like little soldiers with our attention focused straight ahead. After that, our exercise, known as physical education in the schools today, began. After we completed exercise we started our counting drill. This was a method used to make sure that our listening skills were intact. Students had to listen carefully to insure that when it was their turn they knew what their number was. If, by any chance, you missed your number, then you were immediately snatched out of line and punished. The punished student received five good whacks from the switch in Professor Ellis's hand. It wasn't something that any of us wanted to encounter, so the best thing to do was to just pay attention.

The number of students at the beginning of school usually was around one hundred, but after Christmas that number could increase up to three hundred. The real learning day began when we completed our physical education and our numbers drill. A typical school day for students who were in the primer class involved learning to read and write. When your name was called, you proceeded to the board and wrote the alphabet. The Ellis School was a one-room building with a partition that separated the two classes. There was Professor Ellis's class, which was sixth through eighth grade, and Mrs. Paris's class, which was preprimer through fifth grade. The school system was quite different back then. The preprimer, which is known as kindergarten today, is when we were taught how to read. One of the little preprimer booklets we used was entitled *Jack and Jill*. That book was used to determine if we were ready to pass to the next level. If we got past that assignment, we were allowed to move forward to the big primer. When we successfully passed that, we were allowed to enter the first grade. There were many boys in the school who didn't make it past the big primer. It was quite common during those times for children to get discouraged and not finish school. There were many cases where children had to work in order to help provide for the family, and school just didn't fit into the schedule.

Clevester had dropped out by the time I started school. I don't believe he made it past the fourth grade. It was Will Henry, Andrew, Viola, and me trying to learn as much as we could in order to prepare for a life away from the cotton field. Momma made sure that Sister was in charge of us receiving our lunch. Momma would pack biscuits in a lunch bucket and tie a colored string on it. It was a method used for us to identify our lunch bucket from those of the other children. Each day at 11:30 a.m. Professor Ellis would pick two girls to pass out the lunch buckets. Once Sister identified our bucket, she would gather us around. We eagerly followed behind her to the corner of the building and patiently waited for her to issue us our biscuits. There were many times that we received a biscuit and a half with salt meat between the biscuits. It all depended on what Momma could squeeze into that bucket.

The girls always conducted themselves in a respectful manner during lunchtime, but the boys behaved quite differently. The ones who couldn't afford to bring a lunch would gather around you like a pack of wild dogs and beg for your food. In order to eat in peace, Will Henry, Andrew, and I would have to run and hide. There was a pecan orchard behind the school and during the winter many of the children would pick pecans and eat them for a meal. It was a very sad situation having to guard your food, but many children were famished. Their hunger triggered drastic measures. My lunch was taken away from me a few times by the older boys when no one was around to protect me. It brought tears to my eyes, but I believe those tears were more from having to see people that I knew suffering in such a tragic way.

We began preparing for our end of the school year commencement in March. Each child participated by reciting a speech or by having a part in the school play. Everyone from the plantation would be in attendance to witness our performance. The evening of the commencement was fun, but preparing for it wasn't too pleasant. We were required to rehearse every Friday afternoon and not knowing your part resulted in severe consequences. When it came to being disciplined by Professor Ellis, it didn't matter if you were a boy or a girl. He showed no partial treatment when it came to using the switch that stayed constantly in his hand. His only concern was making sure that we all knew what was expected of us when commencement time rolled around. I can remember many nights feeling anxiety leading to the actual event. I cried to Momma and Sister to assist me in making sure I knew my part. There was absolutely no way that I wanted to suffer Professor Ellis's wrath or the embarrassment that came along with not following his strict rules. I made it my business to do well on that night. I had no idea that I was learning a valuable lesson at an early age. Those experiences taught me that I could be proficient in anything that I put my mind to.

The next few years consisted of a combination of going to school a few months out of the year and picking cotton the remainder of the time. I was always alert and very much engaged, which helped me to catch on to some things quickly. It didn't appear that I was learning very much, however, because I struggled with reading and writing. When I reached the sixth grade in 1947, I was able to find employment. I stopped going to school during that time to become a financial contributor to my family. The Malouf family was a white family that owned a store, though they were not planters. Their business was located approximately four miles south of Greenwood, adjacent to the Whittington Plantation. They also began building a motel after the war ended and the construction site increased my responsibilities. My main duty was to carry bricks and cement in a little bucket to the builders. I didn't have the strength at the time to push a wheelbarrow. I cleaned at the store and pumped gasoline and kerosene, but actually I did whatever I was instructed to do. The gas cost only twenty cents a gallon during that time. It seems like those prices never really existed when compared to the cost of gasoline today, but I'm a living witness who can affirm that they did.

My job really came in handy because Poppa received little work during the winter months. I was making eleven dollars a week, which was a pretty decent buck at the time for a country boy my age. Momma was making fifteen dollars a week and my extra pay was a big boost to the family. I loved being able to place the money from my pay in Momma's hand. I was content with receiving only a dollar, which I often split with Andrew. It was a sense of accountability that helped me realize early just how much I enjoyed helping people, especially my family. I was satisfied with the way my life was going. I was a shy country boy with a job and able to keep a little money in my pocket.

It wasn't long, however, before school became an afterthought. I always felt like an outcast in school anyway and now I had a legitimate reason for not going back. The idea of having a job with responsibilities that were quite different from working on the plantation gave me a sense of belonging. I felt I had a purpose and it didn't include struggling to get an education. I always believed that there was never enough time allotted to learning and the short school year did absolutely nothing for my intellectual growth. I wasn't surprised when I failed the sixth grade, but it was enough to gain Poppa's attention. He demanded that I go back to school because my parents still believed that education was a top priority. The following year after we harvested the crops I returned to school. When I walked back into Ellis School there was only one of my siblings left and that was Andrew. Sister was now in high school and once again exposed to a different world that I desperately wanted to be a part of.

Stone Street High School was the name of the school that Sister attended. It was a public school in the city for colored children. High school attendance policies were a little different during those times; students could register for high school in the seventh grade. I completed the sixth grade for the second time and then I decided I wanted to attend school with Sister. Andrew decided that he wanted to stay at Ellis School to complete his education. He was never able to obtain employment which meant he never took a break from his education. I registered for school along with Sister on the first of September. I was rather excited about the idea of being exposed to a different environment away from country living. However, I wasn't allowed to start school until December, despite registering in September. It didn't matter that I was now to attend school in the city; I still had the responsibility of picking cotton on the plantation. I was still considered to be a cotton-picking country boy. The reality was once again shoved in my face that education was secondary for black people.

I will never forget the embarrassment when I walked into the classroom for the first time. The teacher didn't even recognize me and she continued giving me peculiar looks while she questioned my recent whereabouts. She wanted to know where I had been and what I had been doing since September. At first I didn't answer because the classroom was so quiet and all eyes were fixed on me. When she asked again, I softly replied, "I've been picking cotton." I immediately blocked out the snickering from my classmates and diverted my attention to the teacher. She saw the shame in my eyes and didn't bother pressing the issue. I did my best to avoid eye contact as I found an empty chair to occupy. I finally relaxed and looked around to see that all the students were taking an exam. I felt completely lost because I had absolutely no idea about what was going on. I came to understand that the students were taking the six-week test. It was an exam administered to students twice in a semester. It is commonly known today as a midterm and a final exam. I felt totally defeated at that moment because I realized that I had missed too much to possibly catch up on. It was an atmosphere very different from going to school in the country because this school was truly focused on educating black children. The school had a library to increase our reading abilities and an auditorium where plays were held. There was also a shop to train the students for blue-collar jobs. This school was extremely rich in teaching history and it was here that I learned about so many African American icons. I was educated about people such as Frederick Douglass, Richard Wright, and W. E. B. Du Bois, along with many others, and the impact they had on our history. I also saw something that I had never seen before and that was black people in authority. I was elated to see blacks in a light that didn't just consist of picking cotton for "the master."

The principal of the Stone Street School was a man by the name of L. H. Threadgill. He played such an influential role in the Mississippi Delta educational system. His role was later recognized when a school was built and named in his honor. The students in the Stone Street School had an opportunity to change classes each period. We were able to see a different face educating us on a different subject in a different classroom. My new school setting opened me up to real possibilities for the first time and increased my thirst for knowledge. It was the beginning in navigating the direction in which I wanted my life to go. The reason that Sister had always been sent to live with Miss Hattie Sheppard was because of the greater opportunities available at the school. My parents decided that since I was now attending school with Sister there was no reason for her to continue to stay away from home.

We woke up bright and early to start our journey to school. It was an hour-and-a-half walk and we made our way no matter what the weather conditions were. There were many instances when someone pulled over and gave us a ride into town, but if not, we just continued on. We usually arrived early and it was a good thing that we were able to wait at the nearby Diamond Café until school started. The owner of the café knew that we were country children and it was obvious that she felt remorseful about our circumstances. It was also an opportunity for us to get ourselves together because in many instances going to school wet from the rain was quite embarrassing. I remember students laughing when they observed me drying off on the radiators at school. They appeared to get gratification from shouting out that I was a country boy. We were teased and caught smack dead in the middle of humiliation just because of our desire to advance. The families in the country who didn't have children going into town were jealous of us. The white people definitely didn't like it because they wanted to keep us stagnant. It was a constant struggle for blacks to seek education and determination was definitely the key to us staying on track.

Most of the children arrived for school around 7:45 a.m. and classes began at 8:00 a.m. sharp. Sister was already in the ninth grade and most of her acquaintances were in the same class. I failed the seventh grade because I missed the first semester and I received failing grades for the second semester. The word *detained* was placed on my report card at the end of the school year. I was two years behind, but it didn't stop me from keeping a close eye on Sister. I made sure I was right on her heels because she was focused on capitalizing on every opportunity that became available. She was also a classmate of a young girl by the name of Christine Bell who had captured my attention.

I kept my job at the store by working the evening shift and on weekends. It wasn't an easy task but I had become accustomed to having a little change in my pocket. I would rush home from school and immediately prepare for work. I made it in when the sky was pitch black, but I still cracked open the books. It didn't matter how late I stayed up studying, I was up early the next morning preparing for school. As I look back, I realize that this experience was pivotal in my learning responsibilities at an early age. I took pride in maintaining a job and it was instrumental not just in providing me a paycheck. There were two incidents that happened to me at work that were life changing. At the time I felt terrible because there wasn't anything I could do about them, but they long remained a part of my consciousness and sparked my drive to want to make a difference in the lives of others.

The Malouf store was in a location where friends and regular store patrons frequently met and turned the visits into an all-day outing. The store sold illegal whiskey, which automatically attracted a consistent crowd. I could read a lot better by now and I knew every whiskey variety and other liquor labels the store sold. The cars would pull up, the occupants place their order, and I would run into the store and bring the items back to the vehicles. The whites would usually tip me a nickel or a dime. There were occasions when I received as much as a quarter or fifty-cent tip. The potential tip money was great incentive for me to outhustle the other workers, so I made sure that when I saw certain cars cruise up I beat everybody else out in order to get the sale. In the fall, many blacks would come to the store to purchase their groceries. It was during that time that blacks received payment for their cotton picking duties. The women would grocery shop for the needed household items while the children enjoyed the rare treat of some nickel candy. The men gathered around the back of the store socializing and drinking liquor. The black men would put their money together to buy alcoholic beverages, usually a brand named Monroe for $1.25 a half pint. They would then proceed behind the store into a tractor shed to drink. In the summertime the crowds increased and the amount of liquor consumed also increased. Usually they would scrape up enough money to get at least three or four pints and by the end of the day they were intoxicated.

One Saturday afternoon, James Wallace, nicknamed High Stepper, got really drunk. I had just finished serving beer to a white couple parked outside when High Stepper came staggering from the tractor shed. His speech was noticeably slurred as he attempted to tell his wife that he was ready to go. He gained the attention of all the white people as they shook their heads in disgust, watching him stagger around the store. High Stepper and his family left the store and headed in the direction of home. His wife and children carried the grocery bags because he could barely keep his balance. They passed by the white couple's car that I had recently served and High Stepper accidentally rested his hand on the car trunk. The white man quickly jumped out, and this immediately gained my full attention. The white fellow didn't say a word, but suddenly began kicking High Stepper and he wouldn't stop. He was stomping him as if he was literally trying to stomp him into the ground. He knew that High Stepper was intoxicated and wasn't conscious of his actions. It became so intense, so brutal and frightening, that High Stepper's family started begging for his life. His children cried out, "Please don't kill our daddy! Please, mister, don't kill our daddy!" The white assailant appeared not to have an ounce of sympathy for High Stepper and his family. He stormed into the store and rushed up to the owner. He shouted out, "Give me your gun! I want to kill that son of a bitch!" By now High Stepper's family was doing everything in their power to get him off the ground and they just about had to drag him, literally, down the road. The owner refused to give up his gun, which was a good thing because it gave High Stepper and his family more time to get out of harm's way. They were all sweating and horrified as they ran down the road dropping their groceries. They were entirely too scared to turn back and pick up the food that they probably desperately needed to get through the season.

I had never witnessed such a senseless and violent act before. Poppa had told me of incidents of this nature that he had seen, but I never believed that I would see this kind of brutality with my very own eyes. I had an enormous amount of compassion for this black family and having to watch them degraded and pleading for High Stepper's life was something I never forgot. I couldn't believe how this man was kicked like he was a wild animal and how it almost turned into another terrible and senseless black death. I realized that alcohol triggered High Stepper's behavior, but still that type of beating had no justification whatsoever. It also made me realize just how deeply entrenched was the hatred for African Americans. I knew then that I didn't want to grow up and witness such horrible acts of racial brutality and do nothing to try and prevent them.

The second incident that occurred at the store was confirmation that I was going to stay in the state of Mississippi and do everything in my power to change the place that I called home. I was at work and having a mild day when a car with a few white men drove up. I was rather thin for my six-foot frame, and my one-hundred-pound weight made me appear like I was a timid young boy. I went to the car to get their order and realized that I knew two of the men. They were high and obviously itching to start a confrontation. They both looked me up and down and one of them said, "You're that smart son of a bitch!" The statement was made simply because they were aware that I was attending school. It was no secret that white people had a serious problem with black people seeking an education. They said to me again, "You're that smart son of a bitch!" I remained silent because I didn't quite know how to respond to that comment. The driver then grabbed me tightly by the collar and asked, "Do you hear me talking to you?" I was starting to get nervous so I quickly responded, "Yes, sir." The passenger who was a plantation owner jumped out of the car and said, "Teach that son of a bitch a lesson!"

The driver began striking me in my face over and over again. At the same time, he forced me to continue saying, "Yes, sir!" There was nothing that I could do because he had a tight grip on me as he repeatedly punched my face. Everyone looked on as my pride and dignity were stripped away simply for being a black student. I was hit enough in the face to become numb and I actually saw stars for a brief moment. I was finally released after they felt that I had learned my lesson. Everyone went on with their day, including me, but I never forgot that incident. I had nightmares about it constantly and I vowed that I would not be silent concerning issues that strongly affected me and my people.

I continued working and going to school and I stayed focused in order not to repeat another grade. I was already two years behind and I didn't want to be held back anymore. I was tall for my age and I didn't want to become discouraged. Although I felt deep down inside that I could learn anything I applied myself to learning. I was already slightly embarrassed because I wasn't in the same class with the young lady who had captured my attention. Sister had a few classmates who wanted to meet me, but I was shy and I really didn't know how to talk to girls. I felt that Sister's friend Chris was different; there was something about her that was special. I guess one of the things that I liked about her was how she communicated with me, which made me immediately feel comfortable around her. Chris would come by my classroom with one of her friends to get a nickel for a peppermint candy to put inside a pickle. I remember very clearly the evening that I received confirmation that Chris had developed the same feelings for me that I had developed for her. There was a basketball game scheduled one night and I had to work that evening, but I was supposed to get off at nine, which would give me a chance to make it there before the game ended. There was no gym for black students, but we were allowed to play at Wesley Methodist Church. There was a section designated on the second floor where the blacks played basketball. I concluded my workday and caught a ride back to town. I spotted Chris in the stands and I strolled up to her and patiently waited for her to acknowledge my presence. I was rather nervous and I thought the most polite thing to do was to ask her if she wanted anything from the snack stand. She asked for a candy bar. I placed my jacket down in the seat next to her and went to get it. I was shocked when I returned to see that Chris was wearing my jacket. I knew from that moment that she was going to be my girlfriend. It didn't seem to matter to her that I was two years behind in school grade. I asked Chris if it would be okay if I walked her home after the game. I could tell by her expression that she was more than happy to accept my offer. On the way home we passed a place called the Snow Ball Stand. It was a little hall where everyone went to dance. I couldn't dance, but Chris went in and danced while I waited for her to return. She inquired about my age as we continued our walk to her house. She found out that I was exactly one year older than she was. It was also a twist of fate to discover that we were born on the exact same day, which was April 3. Chris couldn't believe it and actually I was rather surprised as well. She went home to tell her mother because our birthdays were approaching. Her family was planning a birthday dinner for her and I was invited. I wanted to come and be around the young lady who gave me goose pimples and brought a smile to my face, but I was extremely shy. When that day arrived, I spent the time alone, sipping on a ten-cent float and thinking about Chris. She was quite disappointed that I didn't show up for the festivities, but she didn't stay angry very long. We were soon reunited and enjoying one another's company. I liked the time I was spending with Chris because it was giving me something to look forward to. I felt deeply in my soul that something really magical was about to happen between the two of us!

Till Death Do Us Part

It was starting to be clear that my feelings for Chris were growing stronger by the day. I not only enjoyed her company, but I also felt quite comfortable in her presence. She was a smart, focused young lady with goals beyond my imagination. It didn't seem to bother Chris that I was still a shy country boy. It was becoming quite evident with each passing day that she was looking beyond the surface. Chris understood that the circumstances surrounding my upbringing had played a major role in developing my character. I was a country boy raised on a plantation and I was shy because I hadn't been exposed to very much. I knew deep down inside that I would have to come out of my shell if I ever wanted to broaden my horizons. Chris was instrumental in helping me break through some of the barriers that came along with country living. It was also a great boost to be attending a school in the city.

I was building my confidence and overcoming the doubt that sometimes overwhelmed me in unfamiliar situations. It was obvious when I opened my mouth to talk that I was born with a gift of gab. I was a young man, in my adolescence, but I was handling business like a grown-up. The thought of being the baby in the family suddenly didn't feel like a reality. I was a sixteen-year-old boy determined to keep some money in my pocket, and one of the main reasons was so I could continue dating Chris. My job was the edge that I had on most young men around my age. I could spend quality time with Chris while enjoying things that most teenage boys couldn't afford. We were able to take in a movie, sip on floats, and enjoy other activities that brought us so much happiness. I didn't allow dating to interfere with my schoolwork because there was no way that I was failing another year. I was already big and tall for my school year and Chris, being two grades ahead of me, already made our experiences quite different. She was just a step away from pursuing her profession and entering into the real world. She never once made me feel a difference in our relationship because I was two years behind in school. I think if it crossed anyone's mind at some point, it was mine. Chris and I gave each other a balance in the very beginning of our relationship. We weren't going to allow our differences to keep us from focusing on what really mattered. We enjoyed being with each other and we learned early what it meant to develop a partnership. I was starting to believe that this girl was made especially for me. It was certain that sharing the same birthday was just one of the many significant things we had in common. Chris was a patient young lady and I could look into her eyes and see that she sincerely cared about me. It's true what's said about the eyes being the window to the soul because I saw something quite defining each time I looked into Chris's eyes. Her eyes spoke so many unspoken words that it inspired me to write a song for her I entitled "Because of Your Eyes I Fell in Love with You." The depth of my feelings for Chris made the lyrics come together naturally in my mind. Writing the song came to me so easily that I decided that I wanted to pursue a music career. I sent off to have music put behind the lyrics and the song was actually played at school. At first I was slightly embarrassed, but then I realized that perhaps a hidden talent had been discovered. The song was confirmation that Chris had captured my heart. It brought us closer together, but it didn't shield us from experiencing the ups and downs that occur when two people are trying to maintain a relationship.

When I reached the eighth grade, Andrew came to join me at Stone Street High School for his ninth year. He decided to complete his education in the country and come to the city when high school actually started. I was glad to have him by my side again as we hiked to school before the crack of dawn. It was like old times and it also gave me a sense of protection knowing that my big brother was once again within shouting distance to me. I had learned a great sense of responsibility being by myself for the first time. Although Sister was in the same school, it was quite different from being with one of my brothers. Sister and I were extremely close and I enjoyed the time we spent together, but there were just certain things that I couldn't share with her that I could with another young man. Andrew had a hard time making the adjustment and he didn't pass the first semester. By the first of December, he was being drafted into the army to serve in the Korean War. I was in the army reserves and I requested a deferment to keep from being drafted. I was lucky, but there was nothing that could keep Andrew from going.

Poppa decided after Andrew was drafted that it was time for us to move. Andrew was always the best one in the family for picking cotton and now with him gone there was no way that we could keep up with the volume needed to earn a decent living. The word spread around the plantation like a wildfire that Cleveland Jordan was packing up his family and moving. We cleared only three hundred dollars from our hard cotton picking duties to use for moving expenses and our new home. It was like a breath of fresh air to know that we were finally moving off the plantation. We moved into a little house in Greenwood that rented for five dollars a week. It wasn't a big home, but it didn't matter because we were in the city now, around civilization. I still maintained employment in the country at the Malouf store and after school I would hitch a ride to work.

When I reached the ninth grade, Morgan Freeman and a few other guys enrolled in the school that I attended. It was common back then to be moved up according to one's height. I was tall, like those boys, and it wasn't long before we quickly formed a bond. Morgan and I remained classmates from the ninth grade through the twelfth grade. Morgan was a very mischievous young man, but he was extremely talented. It was evident during his acting roles in our school plays that he was not just gifted as an actor but could think well on his feet. I remember a play with a cast of Morgan, me, and six other students. The auditorium was filled to capacity with family, friends, and fellow students. The first and second acts were performed to perfection, but things unraveled in the third act. One of the students in the play forgot his lines and his character fainted prematurely during the performance. Our English teacher, who was also the director of the play, became quite nervous. She panicked and demanded that Morgan go onto the stage and attempt to cover up the mistake. Morgan rushed to the stage and quickly developed a new character. He ended the play with an impromptu performance and the audience never knew the difference. We received a standing ovation. It was certainly no surprise to me when Morgan Freeman went on to become a prominent Hollywood actor.

There was another incident involving Morgan that to this day still brings a smile to my face. It was homecoming time and we were having our annual parade in downtown Greenwood. The principal of the school, Mr. Threadgill, would demand that all students be on the best behavior during this event. All the attention was focused on the activities, until Morgan decided to orchestrate another plan. He showed up riding through the parade with his old dilapidated bicycle that had no fenders on the front or back. The handlebars sat in an upright position. He wore a sweatshirt over his head with two holes cut into it that revealed only his eyes. He rode right past the principal, who was livid over the affair. Mr. Threadgill pulled out his strap and began swinging at Morgan as he chased him down the street. Morgan was forced to jump from his bicycle and start running, moving at extraordinary speed. The incident immediately distracted everyone from the parade; I will never forget the humor from that moment. Morgan was a real prankster who loved to keep our algebra class laughing with his jokes. He always had his hand out asking me for a nickel to purchase a pickle. Morgan was excellent in band, diverse in his musical talent in various ways. In my opinion, he is the best in show business and I wish him continued success.

Chris and I continued our relationship, but we broke up a couple of times and tried dating other people. Our separation never lasted long before we always found our way back to each other. It was as if we were destined to be together and it was obvious that we were madly in love with each other. By the time I made it to tenth grade, Chris was preparing to graduate and embrace a new challenge of entering college. She enrolled at Mississippi Valley State College (now Mississippi Valley State University) to pursue a career in nursing. When I reached my senior year of high school, Chris got a job as a nurse in Clarksdale, which is approximately forty-five minutes away from Greenwood. She was definitely pursuing her dreams, but it didn't affect the close bond that we had developed. The way Chris faced responsibilities without hesitation inspired me. It definitely gave me something to look forward to upon completing my high school education.

When I reached eleventh grade Andrew was released from the army. He had served two years in the war and he returned home to pursue his education. Andrew decided that instead of attempting to enroll back in high school he would acquire his GED and then attend college.

During this period of my life there were many incidents of cruelty and discrimination affecting African Americans. I thought leaving the plantation would be a major opportunity for me to move in a different direction, but the environment in race relations appeared to be getting worse instead of better. African Americans were tired of being mistreated simply because of the color of their skin and it was already at the place where critical black voices advocating change needed to be heard. I still vividly recall witnessing those brutal acts of racism at the Malouf store, and how they changed the course of my thinking about racial issues. I wanted to be one of the voices that perhaps could make a difference. I was no longer afraid to speak out about such intolerable and inexcusable issues.

I made a speech in my senior year that surprised my classmates and earned me an A from my teacher. It was an emotional speech and I emphasized with each word the importance of what I wanted to get across. The norm across the country seemed to be the toleration of racial segregation in public schools. There was supposed to be equal treatment when it came to the schools within the districts, but of course that wasn't the case. The black children's educational needs were by no means being met equally with what the white students were receiving. It didn't matter that the black kids had a thirst for knowledge and simply wanted the same opportunities that were available to white children. It was a battle for African Americans to receive to any extent a formal education, regardless of its quality.

The move to remedy the inequities grew out of the epoch case *Brown v. Board of Education, Topeka, Kansas.* The NAACP, long recognized as the leading organization nationally working to improve black civil rights, had brought the case to the highest court in 1954. There it successfully argued that racially segregated public schools violated the Fourteenth Amendment rights of black children, and consigned them to a racial system that perpetuated an inferior status with poor educational opportunities, and hence, life advancement. This case was the initial giant step towards beginning the desegregation of southern public schools. It was also a major breakthrough for me in discovering that I wanted to be part of a solution in putting an end to racism. I was more than happy to deliver a speech on what proved to be such a life-changing topic. When I look back, I realize the speech was the beginning of my personal journey to fight for equality. I had gained the respect of my teacher and classmates by speaking out on a topic that I was passionate about. Moreover, I realized that I had the ability to capture the attention of many people by addressing issues that were strongly affecting the African American community.

When I graduated from high school, I had no idea of what was actually next in my life. I definitely wanted to pursue my education, but I didn't have the money to attend college. I no longer had the luxury of a job, so it became a scary time for me. It was a big accomplishment for me to finally complete my high school education, but I didn't want to end up with scraps and barely making it, especially with Chris being so determined and focused. There were many things uncertain during that time, but one thing that hadn't changed was my commitment to Chris. It had become quite serious between us and she wanted to get married. She actually said that I was going to lose her if I was not interested in marrying her. I was surprised by her comments, but probably more afraid of the responsibilities that came along with such a serious commitment. I didn't know if I was quite ready for marriage, but deep down inside I knew that I didn't want to lose the only woman I had ever loved. I decided that I was going to take it one step at a time and soon the first order of business was obtaining a marriage license.

Poppa and a group of men would often load up the truck and leave Greenwood to haul hay. I decided to tag along with the intent of making some money. I made five dollars, which was just enough to get a marriage license. It was June 9, 1954, that Chris and I were married and I felt in my heart when we exchanged vows that we were going to be together until death do us part! We didn't have a place to stay so we moved in with Chris's mother. I now had the responsibility of a wife and I needed to find employment quickly in order to move us into our own home. I left Mississippi headed to Wisconsin to pick peas and ended up staying for six weeks. It put a little money in my pocket, but certainly not enough to do all the things that I needed to do.

Andrew volunteered to pay my tuition for the first semester of college. The day that I tried to enroll in school, Andrew gave me ten dollars, but unfortunately that wasn't quite enough. I appreciated his good gesture of looking out for his younger brother like he had always done. I was a grown man now with a wife, however, and I knew it was my sole responsibility to make my own path. I finally gained employment as a dishwasher at the Greenwood Holiday Inn. My first check went toward enrolling me in Mississippi Valley State College, located approximately seven miles west of Greenwood. I would get up extremely early to hitchhike a ride, as I did going back in the afternoon. Occasionally, I would pay someone six dollars a week to transport me, but most of the time I didn't have any money. I was determined not to miss school or work, however, so I did whatever was necessary to get to both sites.

Chris was now pregnant and expecting our first child. She was also still working, contributing significantly to the household income. Thankfully, her job as an LPN was pretty secure. Indeed, finding employment in the nursing field was not a difficult task. I was making approximately twenty-five dollars every two weeks as a dishwasher. I always could catch on pretty quickly and my district manager certainly had his eye on me. He knew that I was a swift worker, but he also knew that I was a college student. He recognized my diligence and hard work to do well at both tasks and I'm sure he saw a determined young man. He eventually approached me and said, "Well, you are a college student and I'm sure you can catch on fast." He knew I could run the dishwasher machine with my eyes closed, which made him move me up to a position as salad boy. I always embraced new challenges and new experiences and we definitely could use the extra three dollars that I was now receiving. I made all the combinations of green salads imaginable. I was faster than anyone when it came to making salads because I deliberately attempted to make myself indispensable. I worked from 4 p.m. to 10 p.m. and I made sure that I was always on time. I knew that I was being watched and I was hoping that I could get another raise. I had already decided that I was going to go to school year-round so I could hurry up and complete my education.

My first child was born in 1955 and we proudly made him my namesake. I had a son now, David Jordan Jr., which gave me extra incentive to provide a better life for my family. Chris eventually returned to work as a nurse, having found a job at Greenwood Leflore Hospital. It was a good setup because she no longer had to travel the distance that she previously had, especially less stressful because of the late hours we both kept. My mother-in-law babysat David while we worked and that continued even after we got our own place.

The district manager once again was looking to promote me to another position. He had a conversation with the head cook, whose name was Josh, and asked him if he thought I was ready to make sandwiches. Apparently Josh gave him a favorable opinion of me so I moved into that position, and I was now making $38 every two weeks. Chris was making approximately $115 a month. We decided that it was now time to move into our own place. We were able to purchase some used furniture and get a two-room house. We were doing okay with our combined salary of $191 a month, but we still received occasional help from our folks. It was a blessing that we were able to find a place right down the street from where Chris's mother

Mid-Mississippi Regional Library System.
Attala, Holmes, Leake, Montgomery
and Winston Counties

lived. I got off work before Chris and that allowed me to pick David Jr. up and put him to bed.

Our hectic schedules did not restrict me from keeping up with my studies. I decided that I would seek a degree in science. I was always fascinated with science, and since my musical career didn't get off the ground, this was my second choice. I was enrolled in a lot of chemistry classes and they were quite difficult. Classes started at 9:00 a.m. so I would get up at 6:30 a.m. to try and study. There were only a few students in the class so the courses were not overly challenging because of size. But I had a woman chemistry teacher instructing one of these classes and she graded me extremely hard. She would put so many red marks on my paper that it looked as if my school assignment had been in combat. I would study until 3:00 a.m. because I was determined to pass this chemistry class. I couldn't get discouraged, although the teacher always had negative comments to make about my work. I knew getting limited rest could not be used as an excuse for failing this class. I continued working extremely hard because I realized that in order to earn a science degree core courses like math and physics would have to be subjects that I mastered.

I felt that we were making progress, but 1956 had been a rough year. Moving in the right direction, Chris and I were both diligent workers with goals that we knew were attainable if we worked together as a team. I must admit that this was one of the qualities that made me adore my wife. It was a real asset to our relationship that she was a team player. She was my backbone in keeping me motivated and that made it easy to get through the difficult times. I wasn't getting a lot of rest and money was often extremely tight. I barely had a decent pair of shoes to wear, but I didn't allow that to discourage me. My family meant everything to me and all the sacrifices being made were worth every bit of discomfort I endured.

I was still haunted by the incidents of racial discrimination that had been so troubling to me when I was a young man. It was hard to forget, mainly because the mistreatment of African Americans wasn't getting any better. I was moving more and more in the direction of finding out what I could do to improve the shameful conditions of black people. I thought about the inspiring speech that I made to my classmates right before I left high school. I was extremely proud of myself for educating people on a topic that I felt blacks needed to know about. I think one of the major reasons that we were treated so badly was because of white fear of our power. We have no idea how efficacious a race we really are and even back then we possessed an intimidating presence. Many whites wanted us to remain ignorant about what was transpiring in the world. I believe it was the main reason that white people didn't want us to get the same opportunities when it came to an education. I was starting to view things quite clearly on where we stood as a race and what it was going to take to overcome some of the obstacles that we faced. I wanted to play a role in making some significant changes and I was willing to commit myself to it, totally. I finally received an opportunity to get a close look at what African Americans were really up against in this world because of what some considered the most heinous crime committed in the Deep South. This crime would be the turning point for African Americans in moving to change their dire life conditions and I was more than ready to attend the historical trial that changed the nation!

The Emmett Till Trial

The last of the hot sizzling summer days were quickly dwindling away. The children would soon be back in the classroom and summer vacation would be nothing but a memory. The summer of 1955, however, wouldn't be that easy to forget because a fourteen-year-old black boy was brutally murdered, his death arousing the consciousness of America. His crime was flirting with a white woman and his punishment was something the world would never forget. It was August 28, 1955, and a young boy by the name of Emmett Till was visiting the state of Mississippi. Emmett's mother, Mamie Till, and his grandmother were quite hesitant about Emmett visiting their native home. It was probably because they knew it would be a far different way of life than what he was accustomed to in his hometown of Chicago. Emmett was drilled before he got on the train on what behavior was deemed appropriate in one of the most racist states in the nation. Mrs. Till wanted to be sure that he understood the Mississippi rules, written and unwritten. He was told to say, "Yes, sir, no, sir!" He was told not to look white people straight in the eye and to speak only when spoken to. Mrs. Till prayed that these simple rules would not be too difficult for a city kid who wasn't too familiar with country living.

When Till arrived in the small town of Money, Mississippi, it wasn't long before he was the talk of the town. His outgoing personality and fine dressing quickly put him in the spotlight. There is no telling how many evil eyes were watching this innocent fourteen-year-old boy because the eyes of hatred, racism, and ignorance were quite visible during this time. Unfortunately for Till, something far more sinister than just being watched by evil eyes was about to become his fate.

It was a casual trip to Bryant's Grocery Store for candy and bubblegum that turned out to be the beginning of a senseless murder. Emmett Till allegedly was involved in some kind of inappropriate behavior with the storekeeper, a white woman. A "wolf whistle" was heard reportedly coming from his mouth, but Mrs. Till stated that Emmett sometimes whistled as a means to overshadow a speech impediment. Regardless of the reason for the whistle that afternoon, it caused young Emmett to lose his life. He was dragged out of his uncle's home several nights later and never again seen alive. He was considered missing until his distorted body was found floating in the Tallahatchie River. It was a body totally different from the one that had shown up for summer vacation. Emmett's head was severely bashed in and his face was bloated like that of some fictitious movie monster. His eye was detached and one of his ears was missing. Mrs. Till insisted that his body be returned to Chicago. She wanted her son viewed in his casket in the terrible condition in which he had been found. It was a public observance that drew tens of thousands of viewers. *Jet* magazine displayed the photo of the corpse for those unable to attend the public viewing and they had to print thousands of copies to meet demand. The black community was outraged and desperately wanted to see justice served. Her decision to have an open-casket funeral sent a strong message to African Americans that it was time to take a stand.

I was a freshman in college when the Emmett Till case went to trial. My social studies instructor gave us an assignment that consisted of reading the newspaper in order to follow the proceedings of the trial. We were told to bring in a report from the articles that we read. At the time there were four of us hanging together and one of the guys had a vehicle. Often my brother Andrew, Samuel, T. J., and I sat around discussing the trial. We soon decided that we wanted to do more than just read about the litigations; we wanted to attend. The trial was being held in Sumner, Tallahatchie County, Mississippi, a change of venue for the men accused of Emmett's murder. Two half-brothers, Roy Bryant and J. W. Milam, were charged with this senseless act of violence.

We arrived at the courthouse, the yard filled with spectators and a large contingent of the news media crowding the entrance. We stood outside for a while just to scan the surroundings. I think we still had not gotten over the thought that we were about to be up close to such a historic case. It wasn't long before a beautiful woman made her way through the crowd with a very distinguished gentleman by her side. A reporter quickly pointed the woman out. He shouted, "That's Mamie Till. She is the mother of Emmett Till!" Of course, all eyes immediately shifted in the direction of Mrs. Till. I remember thinking how this must be an incredibly strong woman. She had sent her only son to visit relatives and he had returned to her in a pine box.

Mrs. Till stated that the condition of Emmett's body was so grotesque that she couldn't believe that the sickening sight was her own flesh and blood. I watched the reporters quickly swarm around Mrs. Till. One of the reporters abruptly asked, "Are you Mrs. Till?" She politely said, "Yes, I am Emmett Till's mother." The next question the reporter asked was "Do you think that Emmett will get a fair trial?" Mrs. Till simply said, "I don't know. I'm just here to observe." Apparently the reporter wasn't completely satisfied with her response and it prompted him to ask the question again. I was impressed with Mrs. Till's poise and it appeared that even the media wasn't expecting such a mild-mannered woman. It was quite obvious that she had suffered a traumatic loss, but she wasn't seeking five minutes of fame with the news reporters. She was there to seek justice from the court for the men responsible for her son's death. Mrs. Till finally introduced the gentleman next to her. She said, "I have with me Congressman Charles Diggs from Detroit." The reporter was completely shocked that this black man held such an important political position. He said, "I didn't know we had a nigga congressman." Congressman Diggs maintained his composure and didn't seem bothered by the insult. He was the first African American to represent Michigan in Congress and he appeared to have a rather reserved demeanor. The reporter asked Congressman Diggs the same questions that he had asked Mrs. Till and his answers were exactly the same. Congressman Diggs stated that he was there to accompany Mrs. Till and he didn't know if Emmett Till's trial would be fair.

I thought back to a time in the cotton field when Poppa spoke about a man by the name of Adam Clayton Powell. He was the first person whom I had heard about of African American descent involved in politics and he was also a Baptist minister. Mr. Powell was the first African American elected to Congress from New York. However, Congressman Diggs was the first black congressman I had ever seen. I admired a man who was willing to go against all odds and become the first to achieve such a goal. It made people like me believe that anything was possible, no matter the color of one's skin. Mrs. Till and Congressman Diggs finally entered the courtroom and the four of us college students were just steps behind them.

We walked inside to what felt like a sauna. It must have been ninety-five degrees inside the courtroom. The only source of air circulating came from the big exhaust fans. One of the fans was positioned near the podium a few feet away from the witness box; the second fan was set out in the arena of the courthouse. Once the attention finally shifted away from Mrs. Till and Congressman Diggs, it seemed that all eyes were on us. I guess the local whites figured four young black men should be somewhere picking cotton. Out of the corner of my eye I saw that Tallahatchie's Sheriff Clarence Strider's beady eyes were scanning us up and down. His huge round face was looking so mean that it was almost frightening.

The courtroom was swamped with reporters from all over the country there to cover the story. There was nationally known Simeon Booker, who was the head of the Washington bureau of *Jet* magazine. Other prominent black media coverage included the *Pittsburgh Courier* and the *Chicago Defender*. Present also were numerous reporters from both northern and southern white newspapers and a handful of correspondents from international journals. The courtroom was racially segregated, black reporters sitting on one side of the room and white ones on the other side. My college group had arrived during a recess period, so we had to find seats four rows behind where the whites sat.

The two accused men acted as if they were on a picnic. They were having a jovial time with their wives and children. They popped open Coke bottles at will to quench their thirst in the hot courtroom. It was definitely not the atmosphere that one would expect at a momentous murder trial of this nature. I felt that it was a mockery of justice because there seemed to be no seriousness in the courtroom. Everybody appeared to be just going through the motions, rushing through the trial in order to get back to business as usual. After the recess Mr. Miller, director of the Central Funeral Home in Greenwood, was called back to the witness stand. Miller was the person responsible for picking up the corpse of Emmett Till. His testimony gave precise details as to the condition of the body when it was pulled out of the Tallahatchie River. Till, he said, had been shot in the head and a cotton gin fan had been tied around his neck with barbed wire. When it was time for cross-examination, the white attorney began drilling Miller and sweat poured profusely from the funeral director's face. It looked as if someone had poured a bucket of water on top of his head. Mr. Miller was a highly respected man in the black community and I hated seeing him so intimidated. He couldn't answer the questions quickly enough before he was being asked another. He responded as expeditiously as he could, still remembering to say, "Yes, sir!" One of the questions asked of Mr. Miller was how did he know that it was Emmett Till's body? There was a popular theory circulating that the death of Emmett Till was a conspiracy inspired by the NAACP and that young Emmett was back in his hometown of Chicago. Mr. Miller stated that there was a ring on Emmett's finger stamped with his father's initials. Mrs. Till later confirmed that she had allowed him to wear it down to Mississippi. She had no idea that it would become an item used to identify her son's disfigured body. This was my first time seeing court action and I was very alert as I watched everything that was transpiring. They adjourned after Mr. Miller's testimony with plans to resume the next morning. We walked out a few minutes before the crowd of reporters left and I could feel Sheriff Strider watching our every step as we exited the building.

We got into our vehicle and headed back to Greenwood. Witnessing this trial firsthand had been a very interesting experience for me. On the ride home I thought about the cruelty involved in this young boy's death and how the murder and trial were appearing to be taken so lightly. I immediately felt great sorrow when I thought about Mrs. Till, what she had already suffered through and now having to sit through the court proceedings. The thought that few whites seemed really concerned that she had lost her only son was awful. I wanted to see punishment rendered to the two men who obviously had no respect for human life. I couldn't help but think of how Momma would have felt if one of her children was dropped on her doorstep in a box. It was becoming crystal clear to me that I wanted a part in changing the unjust laws, written and unwritten, that affected African American people. It was a terrible act to take this fourteen-year-old boy's life and the guilty needed to pay for their deed. As I thought about the actions that I witnessed in the courthouse, however, I didn't feel confident that justice in this case would be served, as it had not been with so many others where blacks were victims. I remembered my speech on the 1954 Supreme Court decision involving segregated schools, and the effect that speech had on my life. I wanted to be a voice for African American people and sitting in on the trial had put some serious things on my mind.

At first our classmates didn't believe that we attended the trial. The instructor was also a little skeptical about our actual presence at the courtroom proceedings. We were told to give an oral presentation to the class on what had transpired thus far in the trial. We told the story in such a detailed way that we convinced them that we had to have been there. We had everybody's attention and they were hanging on every word. This was the biggest topic going on at the time and it had captured attention even worldwide. Reporting to the class gave me the same sense of gratification that I got from the speech back in high school. I was speaking on a topic that black people desperately wanted to know about. It was common back then for blacks to be quiet and not ask many questions about racial matters. Here I was filling in the blanks to some of the questions that were probably going through their minds.

I also shared with them the information involving the media coverage. I told them about a man by the name of John Popham who was a *New York Times* reporter. Popham was thought to be the only national correspondent at the time assigned full-time to cover the South. He helped set up the protective ground rules for the visiting journalists with this being such a high-profile case. It was agreed that black reporters would stay in Clarksdale, located approximately twenty miles from the courthouse. It was advised that they stay out of Sumner after nightfall because of all the prevailing tension. We shared with the class what we saw as inappropriate behavior displayed inside the courthouse. We discussed the quiet disposition of Mrs. Till and how she had a black congressman by her side during the proceedings. The instructor gave us an A for the presentation because he was also quite interested himself in the information that we shared with our classmates.

On the third day of the trial, the courthouse was again packed with reporters. They were there from all over the country and even outside of the country; a reporter was there from Europe. At first the dozen or so black reporters were refused seats, but after the judge heard requests of support for them from white reporters he decided to let them in. It was amazing to me how there appeared to be one disrespectful situation after another concerning black people. One would have thought after such a brutal killing that the display of racism would not be so blatant during this trial, but to some, including the accused, it didn't matter. The white reporters, however, insisted on a more equitable treatment of their black colleagues and their views added a positive dimension to the quest for justice. One night a few white reporters were summoned to the nearby all-black town of Mound Bayou. There, they were joined by top black reporters and were told by a few locals of potential new witnesses who had not previously come forward because they feared not being taken seriously by white authorities. The reporters, black and white, joined together and formed a team, which Simeon Booker said launched "an incredible interracial manhunt." They spread out across the Delta in hopes of finding other witnesses. They found a teenage field hand who was able to testify to hearing Emmett being beaten for a long time. Other prospective witnesses disappeared, despite the efforts of Mississippi NAACP leader Medgar Evers, who placed his own life in jeopardy by posing as a field hand, a guise to hide his major effort to protect witnesses. Mr. Evers went as far as smuggling a witness out of town in a coffin. The black population was desperately searching for anything or anyone who could shed favorable light on the case. Mr. Wright, the uncle of Emmett, could only testify that the men took Emmett away from his home. His testimony, however, was courageous and quite revealing. He stood up while on the witness stand and pointed out Milam and Bryant as the men who came into his home and kidnapped Emmett. It was unheard of back then to accuse white folks of anything. Pointing a finger directly at them the way he did was definitely not done. Emmett's young cousin, who was present when Emmett was taken, corroborated Wright's testimony. Their testimony proved to be of little effect, however; the defendants had already admitted to kidnapping Emmett, but they claimed to have let him go and had no idea what transpired after that.

The trial lasted five days but it took the jury only sixty-seven minutes to deliberate. The defendants were acquitted by the all-white male jury. The acquitted men stood outside in front of photographers lighting up cigars and kissing their wives to celebrate their victory. After the acquittal, Sheriff Strider issued this statement: "We never have trouble with our niggers until they go north and come back. I guess the NAACP and Chicago niggers are satisfied now!" It was a comment that earned him notoriety. The verdict was an outrage and my heart ached for Mrs. Till because she had lost her only son. She had also lost an opportunity to see justice prevail. The reason given for the acquittal was even more ridiculous. The defense's argument that a body had been planted by the NAACP and passed off as that of Emmett Till simply to stir up trouble was insulting to human decency. It didn't matter that the defendants had admitted to kidnapping Emmett, a major crime in itself. Indeed, the grand jury had refused to indict Milam or Bryant on kidnapping charges, thus totally ignoring the law and reason for this body's existence. I didn't quite understand how all the evidence pointed to guilt, but the defendants' skin color ultimately made them innocent. News of the acquittal of the two men who had Emmett Till's blood all over their hands quickly spread around the world. Some of the headlines in newspapers across the country were as follows: "THE SCANDALOUS ACQUITTAL IN SUMNER" and "THE LIFE OF A NEGRO ISN'T WORTH A WHISTLE." I wondered if a white boy had been kidnapped by black men in the manner that Till was kidnapped how quickly an indictment and guilty verdict would have been handed down. I was angry, bitter, sad, and disillusioned by this entire miscarriage of justice. The issue of *Jet* magazine with photos of Emmett Till's disfigured body was something I vowed to always keep. The whole sordid affair served as an inspiration and motivation for me to continue to place myself in positions where I could challenge the wrongs that constantly affected black people. I had seen with my very own eyes that blacks in positions of authority did exist. I was determined to stay on the path of pursuing justice for my people and fulfilling my sense of a noble obligation.

A few months after the trial, Milam and Bryant confessed to the murder of Emmett Till. Their confession didn't come at the mercy of the court because they were overwhelmed with guilt and wanted to clear their consciences. Instead, their heartless confession was published in a magazine article. The two men obviously were quite familiar with the law and knew that double jeopardy meant they could not be tried for the same crime twice. The article was a payday for them, the confession story supposedly worth four thousand dollars to them. *Look* magazine, one of the most popular magazines of the era, clearly paid a small price to publish the factual events attached to this infamous case.

The black community was already outraged over the whole Till matter and to see the guilty men now boasting about the senseless murder only intensified the anger and disgust. Black people were tired of the persistent injustices and were even more disturbed that white people seemed to feel that a black life had no value or worth.

Black southerners, especially, were being infused by this hostile atmosphere. Two black men who had advocated voting rights for their race had been murdered months before the Till murder trial. Soon after the Till trial ended, Rosa Parks refused to give up her seat on a segregated city bus, launching the historic Montgomery, Alabama, bus boycott. The Till case was quickly becoming the catalyst for the modern civil rights movement!

Stepping into
the Movement

The acquittal of the two men responsible for Emmett Till's death heightened emotion and black activism all over the country. I'm sure the Till affair was something that white folks wished had never happened. They could never have imagined that blacks would react like they did in the trial's aftermath. Anger and frustration prompted them to take a determined stand. It was not like people expected Emmett Till's killers to be executed, but we certainly thought it reasonable for some form of prison punishment to be rendered. During the trial proceedings I had witnessed something that I had never seen in my entire life. I saw the mingling of black and white people in one particular place, the Plaza Hotel, which was the only black-owned hotel in the Delta. It was an establishment with a big lobby where blacks socialized and drank beer. There was also a television there, something that wasn't too common back then, and both races would sit around the lobby and appear to be enjoying the atmosphere. Occasionally, I would stop by after I got off work, around ten at night. I never stayed long, maybe thirty minutes at the most. I would grab a beer and mingle long enough to hear people express bitter opinion about the outcome of the trial. The younger African Americans would discuss the type of revenge they wanted to carry out for this wrong, especially after having had a few beers. We talked in clusters and amongst ourselves, but I always stayed conscious of the time. I made it my business to get home by 10:30 p.m., to keep Chris from fussing. I was a married man with a son and I knew all my free time needed to be spent with my family.

The thought of actually seeing blacks and whites together made me know that it was possible for us to breathe the same air in harmony. I knew that there was no legitimate reason for the deep hatred and racism that African Americans suffered. I felt the difference in skin color should not have been the major factor for denigrating African American people.

There had already been a death, months prior to the Till case, of another black person killed when no one was ever convicted of the crime. A man by the name of Rev. Charles Lee from Belzoni, Mississippi, was murdered for trying to register blacks to vote. The authorities sought to cover up the murder, saying that the death resulted from a car wreck after Lee ran into a telephone pole. Astonishingly, they claimed that gunshot pellets found inside of the car were actually lead fillings from his teeth. All the prominent black state leaders were angry about the police report, including Medgar Evers, the major Mississippi civil rights voice. Even national black leaders expressed outrage over another miscarriage of justice because they knew the real reason behind Lee's death. The tensions emanating from black America made me feel something was about to happen concerning black people and it wasn't long before my feelings became a reality.

It was December 1, 1955, a few months after the Emmett Till trial had ended. The trial was over but certainly not forgotten because it sparked the Montgomery bus boycott. Rosa Parks, popularly known as "the First Lady of Civil Rights" or as "the Mother of the Freedom Movement," became the catalyst in starting this local movement. Like other southern cities, Montgomery adhered to a strict policy of segregated seating on its buses. Whites took seats in the front and blacks sat in the back. In the event that a white boarded the bus, the black person closest to the front would have to give up his seat, and another row for whites would start. Bus driver James Blake had been in a previous incident with Rosa Parks, so the two were familiar with each other. On her ride home one evening Parks and her row of riders were ordered to move back so a white man could be seated and a new row started for white riders. Everyone on Parks's row complied with the driver's order, except her. She refused to give up her seat and was eventually arrested. Her bold refusal and arrest for violating the segregation policy prompted the boycott. The night that Parks was arrested a flyer circulated through the black community. It was a notice encouraging blacks not to ride the buses to work, school, or anywhere else. A new organization, the Southern Christian Leadership Conference (SCLC), emerged to direct the boycott. The head of the organization was a young Baptist minister around thirty years old named Dr. Martin Luther King Jr. He was the one responsible for orchestrating the Montgomery bus boycott and inspiring the participants. Thus, it was Rosa Parks who was instrumental in helping to launch Dr. King to national prominence in the civil rights movement and his eventual rise to international status. Rosa Parks was the secretary of the Montgomery chapter of the NAACP when she was arrested. She once said that Emmett Till's death is what triggered her refusal to give up her seat. We black Mississippians felt good to know that blacks all over the country were willing to avenge the death of a person killed in the Magnolia State.

Mrs. Parks was regarded as a hero in the eyes of African Americans, but it was an honor that came with dire personal consequences for her and others as well. She lost her job as a seamstress and eventually had to relocate to Detroit, Michigan. Dr. King was jailed several times and his home was bombed. King remained resolute, however, determined to continue the effort peacefully, and personally calmed black anger after the bombing. Several church bombings also occurred as violent-prone whites tried to thwart the boycott in the only way they thought they could. The boycott had a crippling effect on the transit system as car pools and black taxis filled the necessary gap in getting blacks to and from their destinations. Many simply walked. For their involvement, numerous boycotters were physically attacked and authorities sought to retaliate against many of them by putting them in jail on bogus charges. It was the most ridiculous thing that I had heard of, the idea of punishing people for using other methods of transportation. Black people were responsible for generating three-fourths of the revenue the public transit system received, so they were in an advantageous situation. Obstacles aside, black Montgomery was not going to be deterred from their cause to break the back of segregated public transportation. There was much at stake, as one lady emphasized when asked why she was walking in support of the boycott. She replied that her feet were tired but her soul was at rest because she was walking for the benefit of the next black generation. This was an example of ordinary people doing extraordinary things to bring about real change. The boycott and the subsequent civil rights movement liberated a lot of African Americans, including me. It influenced me to go on and be elected to the Mississippi state legislature and work to change the condition of my people in my home state.

The boycott lasted for an entire year before the court gave the last word and declared that segregation on city buses was unconstitutional. As it came from the court, anyone could sit wherever they wanted on the bus and it was King who took the first ride, along with a few others. Black people in Mississippi rejoiced over the victory; although we didn't actually participate in the boycott, it was just enlightening to know that blacks were actively making decisions to change the wretched state to which segregation and racism had long confined them. There were many who couldn't believe that African Americans had the courage to actually go forward in not riding Montgomery buses. But they did, and it was this type of action starting to occur in the heart of the South that was instrumental in forcing real social and political changes.

I felt comfortable with my status. I was a working man who was in college and enjoying every minute of both. My wife was extremely smart and our dedication to each other inspired us to continue to move forward as a team. We were making a pretty decent living for a young married couple during those times. We had our own house, although our furniture was old and our radio, an important source of evening and weekend entertainment, seldom worked well. I had a son and that pleasingly ensured that the Jordan name was carried on. I enjoyed still being able to have fun, although a lot of responsibilities weighed heavily on my shoulders. Most of my time was spent in school and work, so I tried to make the best of the fun times just to break the monotony. I was rather mischievous and I really enjoyed pulling pranks on people. I always managed to have fun with my work buddies because it helped make the hours pass. I worked on the evening shift with four African American men and I was the person in charge of making the sandwiches. I was good at what I did and my boss liked me because I was quick in completing what tasks needed to be done.

I always got a big kick out of having a new employee show up and be placed under my wing. The new employee would eventually ask for a sandwich and I always made it my business to make two. One would be loaded with Tabasco sauce, hot peppers, and all other types of spicy ingredients that I could get my hands on. I would garnish it nicely and politely hand it to him. He would take his sandwich and walk off to the dish room thinking that he was about to enjoy a nice meal. It wouldn't be long before I would hear cussing and fussing once he had bitten into the sandwich. There was one incident when a new hire broke a plate because he angrily threw the sandwich down. He hollered, "What the hell did that cook give me?" The other workers and I would burst into laughter and then I would go and give the new person the sandwich that wasn't saturated with the peppery items. I also enjoyed it when a new employee came in and I would give him the wrong duty instructions just for a laugh. For example, I might tell him to go and bring me an oven jack. Of course there was no such object, but he would frantically search for it until someone would ask him what he was looking for. He would be out of breath by the time he was able to tell someone what he was even searching for. Eventually, all the guys would laugh and tell the new employee that he had been sent on a wild goose chase. It was good humorous times like these which helped us, temporarily, block out much of the chaos going on in the world.

My family was also instrumental in helping me to focus on staying on the right track. I wanted to achieve things that I felt would put my family in a better position to enjoy life. Momma was still working at the hotel and making very little money, but she was a determined woman who was no stranger to hard work. I worked extremely hard because I wanted to be able to make things manageable for Momma to enjoy her golden years. Poppa and Will Henry were still picking cotton because they had no trade. They were forced to pick up odd jobs during the winter months to make ends meet. During this time period, cotton trucks would leave Greenwood to take pickers to the field where they worked from sunrise to sunset. The laborers would be paid each day for their cotton picking duties. Once the season ended, Poppa and Will Henry would be in a desperate search to find work. My eldest brother, Clevester, had found himself a new home with no plans on returning to the South. He was now residing in Toledo, Ohio, and working at the Interlake Iron Company. The company made steel and iron, and Clevester was making a pretty decent living working there. I was glad to see that my oldest brother's past difficulties had not hindered him from surviving and prospering in this world. Sister was now married and employed as a teacher in Shaw, Mississippi. She worked there for an extensive period of time before she got a teaching job in the Greenwood public school system. Andrew and I still had a very close relationship as brothers. We were in college together and we were able to hang out with each other when time permitted. Everyone was doing reasonably well taking care of their needs and we still considered ourselves a pretty close-knit family. We all had our own lives, but we managed to keep close tabs on one another.

In the summer of 1956 I made a decision that I needed to attend college all year around. Chris didn't want me to burn myself out, but she was pregnant with our second child and I wanted to accelerate and complete my education in order to get a better job to support my family. I planned to take chemistry during the summer months. This was the subject that I struggled in and I wanted to be sure the course didn't hold me back from receiving my college degree. I was about to acquire another mouth to feed and I knew the added responsibility wasn't going to be easy on me. The baby daughter that we named Joyce was born in October of 1956. There was a thirteen-month difference between the two children, which made it seem as if we had two babies at the same time. Chris took her six-week leave of absence from her job, but she worked up to the time that Joyce was born. During this time we struggled tremendously. We encountered greater expenses because Chris was a knowledgeable nurse and she was determined about the kids getting the very best form of nourishment. I couldn't buy anything for myself, but I considered it to be unspoken sacrifices that had to be made. I had gotten so poor that I was putting cardboard in my shoes. The constant transport to and from school and work had certainly worn the soles of my shoes out. I kept on going despite the many obstacles that I encountered. I knew that every step I took was helping me to put my family in a better situation. I will not pretend that there weren't many times I just wanted to throw in the towel because some days were more difficult than others. I was getting minimum rest and the hours that I had to keep didn't allow my eyes to stay shut too long. However, I thought about all the sacrifices that blacks were making across the country and it made me realize that I was no different from them. It was apparent during these times that nothing easy was going to come to people of color. The movement was still making headlines so black people were still fighting for justice.

In 1957 the NAACP registered nine black students to attend an all-white school in Little Rock, Arkansas, Central High School. These students were selected on the basis of excellent grades and attendance. It was also a way to test the decision from the case of *Brown v. Board of Education, Topeka, Kansas*. This was the case that I once made a speech about. Large numbers of whites in Little Rock tried to block these students from going to school. They were actually attempting to ignore the federal court order that stated that blacks couldn't be discriminated against when it came to attending Central High. Orval Faubus, the governor of Arkansas at the time, called up the National Guard to keep those students from entering the school. The conduct of the irate parents of the white students was appalling, much of their abusive behavior captured on national television news programs. President Eisenhower called a press conference and stated that he wouldn't allow anyone to block the federal court order admitting the students. The president actually delivered a powerful speech, indicating that the students must be protected at all costs. He was forced to send in the armed forces to keep peace and order on the campus. When the army trucks showed up on the scene it was an African American soldier who was the first one to step out. Blacks in Mississippi loved seeing that and it was gratifying to us when we saw the pictures of the federal forces used to stifle white opposition to this latest effort of blacks to eliminate another barrier of southern racism. Some whites claimed that they were struck by black soldiers and, understandably, they did not like it. For the first time I saw blacks being able to use force against white people to maintain law and order. I was especially elated over what I saw. The pictures of black soldiers in combat mode stayed plastered on the wall in one of my college classrooms for quite some time.

The Little Rock Nine were eventually admitted to the school to pursue their education, but it didn't happen without a struggle. It was becoming more evident to me that blacks were ready to defend their positions all over the country. It also appeared that the movement was quickly spreading throughout the Deep South. I became even more intrigued with the civil rights movement because Poppa was now heavily involved in it. He participated in marches and attended many mass meetings held to mobilize black Mississippi. I was interested in all the moves that black people were making. It was becoming more and more of a reality to me that I had to be a part of changing the South. I wasn't really involved in the movement as I would have liked to be and one of the reasons was because I was rock-bottom poor. However, it didn't mean that I wasn't conscious of what was transpiring. I continued my daily routine for the next couple of years. I was strictly focused on graduating from college because I knew a degree would open up more opportunities for me. I did everything in my power to provide a stable environment for my family but I still had my eye on the progress that black people were making and I knew deep down inside that there was going to come a time when I would have to take a decisive step to get involved. I was going to have to be in charge of something in order to get to where I wanted to be!

When Duty Calls

I t was the most glorious day that I can remember. I had reached a milestone in my life, something that at one time I could never have imagined. It was May of 1959 and I was receiving my college degree. I thought back to the day when Andrew gave me ten dollars to enroll in college. It wasn't enough, but I appreciated the great gesture. I had struggled and worked two jobs in order to make this dream become a reality and now I was reaping the benefits from my hard work. The little boy who daydreamed in the cotton field instead of concentrating on picking cotton had beaten the odds and was now receiving a bachelor of science degree, something that could prepare me for a far more fulfilling life. There were approximately forty-nine students in my graduating class and five of us graduated with science degrees. Most of our time had been spent in the lab. I did my major paper on osteology, which is the study of bones. The graduation ceremony was held in the gymnasium at Mississippi Valley State College; I was so happy and excited about it—receiving such a light piece of paper that carried so much weight. My cousin, William Stewart, picked us up for the graduation ceremony, all of my immediate family. I was even happier about the day because my young children would be able to witness my accomplishment. My wife had been very supportive while I pursued my degree and she deserved so much of the credit for being my backbone during this difficult process. I had always felt in my heart that the sacrifices would definitely pay off for me and my family to have the solid future I wanted for us.

I had already been offered a job in the county school district. I would be teaching science to seventh and eighth graders in Minter City, which was twenty-five miles north of Greenwood. All county schools operated on a split session because of the cotton picking season. The schools were out in September and October, which was the time that blacks were on the plantation picking cotton. I went back to my old job at the Holiday Inn and worked part-time until the school session was ready to begin. Our future could not have looked brighter; Chris and I wanted another son, so she was pregnant with our third child. I wasn't worried about being able to provide for my family because I had a teaching job now and Chris was still employed as a nurse. I felt euphoric about life until the first week of June.

It was a summer day in 1959 when I walked to the mailbox and got the worst letter that I had ever received. The letter stated that on June 17, 1959, I was required by federal law to report to Fort Jackson, South Carolina, to enroll in the U.S. Army. I would then begin my required military service of two years. The military service had allowed me to attend school and not go into the army when Andrew was called. I had joined the army reserve in order to get deferred and now they were calling for me. I informed them that I couldn't go on active duty because I had two small children and my wife was pregnant with our third child. Chris was experiencing some slight medical issues with the varicose veins in her legs and she needed me home. The officer with whom I talked had no compassion for my situation and informed me that regardless of my personal circumstances, I needed to be on the scheduled train heading to South Carolina. I remember Chris was at work and I thought about how I was going to break the news to her. I sluggishly walked the few miles to her job thinking that there was no way that I wanted to be away from my family. When I approached Chris, our eyes met and she knew that something was wrong. It was difficult for me to say the words, so I simply handed her the letter. She quietly read it and sadness immediately filled her eyes. I knew that she needed me every step of the way during her pregnancy. We had never spent a long period of time away from one another. It appeared that just when things were looking up for us we were being forced to separate.

I arrived in South Carolina on the date that I was due to report.

It was quite sad having to say goodbye to my family, but I knew that I was going to do everything in my power to return home quickly. The draftees spent one week in South Carolina getting processed; after that we would be dispatched to different locations. I remember the funniest thing happening to me after being there for a couple of days. We had to attend church on Sunday and there we were told that whatever our problems, we should take them to the priest. I was a Baptist and I didn't know anything about confessing to a priest. I looked around and did what I saw everyone else doing. I bowed down and the priest approached me and placed his hand on my back. He asked me what harm had I done during the week that had brought me to the point of making a confession. I told him that I wanted to get out of the army and I was there to see if he would help me get discharged. The priest demanded that I get up and move on because I was seeking help for the wrong thing. When I think back, that was hilarious to me, although at the time I was dead serious about my request.

I received three or four calls at different times about going to Officer Candidate School (OCS). Officials had looked up my record and found out that I had a bachelor's degree in science. I was academically qualified to become a second lieutenant. I remember very clearly that I may have offended one of the officers because I told him that I wasn't interested in going to OCS. He couldn't understand—since I was due to serve two years, why not make the best of it. I never told him that I working on getting a discharge from the army. He was a black officer who tried convincing me of the great opportunity I was passing up. I eventually just had to tell him bluntly that I didn't want to be an officer and I was immediately dismissed.

After the first week, I was shipped off to Fort Hood, Texas, to begin basic training. It was the headquarters for the Third Army, a place soldiers called "Hell on Wheels." I was there with one of my college classmates and I had made a few other buddies during the week. I was happy to know that I was going to Texas because I was getting closer to home. It seemed as if the training instructors would wait until it started raining or the sun was blazing before they called on the soldiers for drills. They would run us all day; I was glad that I was in good shape because I didn't weigh much.

I remember being impressed when I first laid eyes on a black lieutenant. Although at the bottom of the commissioned hierarchy, he was still an officer and this meant he commanded some authority and had to be respected because of it. He asked me, "How tall are you, soldier?" I replied, "Six-two, sir." He said, "Damn, you got the biggest feet that I have ever seen!" My boots were a size thirteen or fourteen even though I wore only a twelve. It was hilarious to me and my buddies because my shoes were pretty big for my weight. Then there was the time the sergeant, who was a Texan, confronted me. He got right up in my face and said, "Jordan, I heard you put in for a damn hardship discharge!" I said, "Yes, sir, Sergeant." He walked away with a cocky strut as if I was wasting my time thinking that the army was going to let me out, but I was determined not to give up my fight to receive a discharge. I finally asked to see the company commander. I explained to him that my wife was pregnant and that she needed me at home. It was peacetime and I saw no reason why I couldn't be at home taking care of my family. I also informed him about the teaching position that I had waiting for me back home. I had his full attention and I could tell that he was carefully listening to every word I said. He looked dead into my eyes and said, "This is the army and your reasons aren't good enough!" However, he informed me that he would send my request to higher authorities because there was nothing that he could personally do for me.

It took about six weeks before I got a phone call from a drill sergeant. He said, "David Jordan, that damn discharge that you put in for came through!" I was extremely happy; indeed I guess I was a little too overjoyed because the sergeant immediately found a way to punish me. He told me to clean the washroom and that someone would give me the equipment that I needed for the job. I was handed a toothbrush and a small bucket and told to get to work. This was my punishment for receiving my discharge, but it didn't bother me one bit. I cleaned the bathroom with that toothbrush from top to bottom and it took me about five hours to finish. I was going home and nothing that they said or did was going to rain on my parade. I couldn't wait to call Chris and tell her the good news. A lot of people had written the army on my behalf in order for me to be released and it had paid off.

There were other soldiers who were being discharged for various reasons and we were held together at the processing station. There was a white soldier among us being discharged who tied his duffle bag to the back of a taxicab. The driver drove off not knowing the bag was tied to the bumper. The soldier stated that he had done this because he didn't want anything from the army or anything that re-minded him of it. We didn't have to participate in any more drills, but we still had chores to do while they were processing our paper-work. I had friends who wanted to make a career out of the army, but I knew that military life wasn't for me. It took a week after re-ceiving the good news to actually leave the army base. We caught a Greyhound bus out of Texas en route to home. When we got to Shreveport, Louisiana, about six soldiers were still left on the bus. We stopped there for a rest period and to grab a bite to eat. We reboarded and tried to sit in our original seats in the front, but we were informed by the police that we had to give up our seats. There were four or five white women who needed to board the bus. We got up and moved to the back, but we did so knowing how unjust this was; indeed, this was a violation of our rights, because the Truman administration had already outlawed the segregation of the armed forces. We were traveling in our military uniforms, but technically we were back in the civilian world. Moving to the back of the bus hurt a little, but I really didn't care that much because I was on my way home. I made it back to Greenwood a couple of days after Labor Day, 1959. It seemed as if I had been gone for years because I truly missed being at home. I was so excited about being back that I actu-ally walked home from the bus station. I could see David Jr. in his swing set outside when I got a few steps from the house. He was the first one to lay eyes on me and the happy reunion started from that point. Chris was really glad to see me and the children couldn't stop asking questions, which let me know that I had been truly missed.

The next day I went to see about the teaching job that had been promised to me before I departed for the army. I was in time to start in November because the black students in the Mississippi Delta were out for cotton picking season. The principal informed me, however, that the position at the county school had already been filled. It was mid-October by now and I was still searching for a job. I had a little money stashed away, but it was quickly dwindling down. One day a black, bald-headed, heavy-set man showed up on my doorstep. I answered the door and the man immediately took off his hat and asked if I was David Jordan. I said, "Yes, sir. How can I help you?" He introduced himself as Mr. Bubble Brown from Indianola and informed me that he was the principal of Gentry High School. I invited him in because I was anxious to know the reason for his visit. Mr. Brown said, "I understand that you recently got out of the army and that you're looking for a job." I quickly said, "Yes, sir. I am." He went on to tell me that he would hire me and I accepted his offer.

I was scheduled to report to Gentry High School on November 3. I was ecstatic and so was Chris, but there was one problem. I didn't have transportation and the school was about thirty miles away from home. So, I needed to address this issue right away. There was a black man by the name of Walter Williams who worked for a local car company and I informed him that I desperately needed a car. At that time only a few blacks in Greenwood bought new cars and I could not afford one either, but I could buy a late model vehicle if it was dependable. I purchased a 1955 black and red Pontiac, which was four years old. My car note was going to be forty-two dollars a month, but I had six weeks before my first payment was due.

I had to take the driver's test so I could get my license. The procedure required the patrolman to ride with the applicant to see how well he did behind the wheel. He took me to a gravel area where, unfortunately, the car got stuck. He asked what would I do to get out of this ditch and I told him that I didn't know. He snatched the gear and said, "Nigga, put the gear in double two!" I was finally able to drive out of what seemed like a sand dune, but I was afraid that I had failed the driving test. The patrolman was extremely quiet all the way back to the station, but he passed me and I was able to get a license. I drove the Pontiac home and my family jumped in and we all went cruising down the street.

I started my first teaching job at Gentry High School as scheduled in November. There were two other teachers who carpooled with me to share on the gas expense. I taught mathematics and science to ninth-grade students. My salary was twenty-two hundred dollars for the seven months from November to May. Most of my students were males from the country who were quite mischievous. I came to realize that a freshman class anywhere would be a force to be reckoned with because of their youth and their status of being in the bottom class in high school. It appeared that I would have no problem adjusting to working at this school. I had only one complaint and that was with Mr. Brown, the type of principal who was tougher on the teachers than he was on the students. I quickly made the adjustments to my new job, but I felt even better knowing that I had options if things didn't work out. I had been offered a job by my old manager from the Holiday Inn to become an assistant manager in St. Louis, Missouri. I turned it down because I had no intention of relocating, but it was a good feeling to know that my hard work ethic had not gone unnoticed. I was quite pleased with the way things were going in my life and then I was hit with some terrible news!

I remember clearly that day in November 1959 that made my heart drop as I listened carefully to the news from my wife. Chris told me that her medical test revealed that she had a spot on her lungs. An old schoolmate of Chris's was in the hospital suffering from tuberculosis and she was waiting to be transferred to the state hospital. Chris went into her room to assist her with something and didn't wear a mask. It was unfortunate that Chris contracted tuberculosis during that short visit. It was a scary time for us because Chris was about six months pregnant with our third child. The severity of the illness required her to be sent to a sanatorium in Magee, Mississippi, which is approximately 130 miles away from Greenwood. My mother-in-law kept the children until I got home from work in the afternoon. I remember the children constantly asking about the whereabouts of their mother. It was a difficult time and if it hadn't been for my mother-in-law I don't think I could have gotten through it. Chris had been away from home for three months now and she was badly missed. I took the kids to see her every two weeks and it always turned into a sad occasion. They were not permitted to go upstairs to see her so she would come to the window and wave to them from there. They were young and didn't quite understand what was happening, so I couldn't wait until the day that we could be together again as a family.

When I walked into the school office on February 1, 1960, the principal immediately informed me that he had just received a phone call from the sanatorium where Chris was a patient. He was smiling as he informed me that Chris had given birth to my son, Donald Jordan. I was extremely excited and I asked if it would be okay for me to leave. Mr. Brown didn't hesitate giving me permission to go be with my family. I drove and picked up my mother-in-law and Samuel Sampson and we headed to Magee. We brought Donald back to Greenwood when it was time to head back. I hated leaving Chris at that hospital because I could see the sadness in her eyes. She had always bonded with the children immediately after their birth and I knew nothing compared to the bond between mother and child. I wanted her to be around the new addition to the Jordan family, but I also knew that she had to be completely cured of the disease before being released. I was going to do the very best that I could to handle things in her absence, but I knew that my mother-in-law really had everything under control. She loved the children with all her heart and I made sure she had everything she needed when it came to providing them with their daily essentials. I thought on the ride home about how I had been called to duty for the army and now I was being called to duty at home.

I had the responsibility of making sure that things stayed intact until Chris returned home. She spent a total of eight months in the hospital, away from the family. When it was time to finally pick Chris up, I was required to go to summer camp. I had been discharged from the army, but I had an obligation to fulfill my two-week duty in the army reserve. I completed my duties and I couldn't wait to return home in order for all of us to be together as a family. It seemed like an eternity since we had all been under the same roof and I was glad to have my wife back at home. She had some recuperating to do and she had to be tested periodically to make sure her lungs were okay, but for the most part she was back to her old self.

Chris getting sick and being away from home had really convinced me about the importance of prioritizing in my life. I wanted her to consider being in a position where she could be in full authority on her job, so I encouraged her to go to college. I borrowed money for her tuition and the rehabilitation company paid for her books. I was making enough money to hold down the household expenses while she attended school. I wanted to assist her in every way possible in obtaining a college degree.

In 1962 the civil rights movement came to Greenwood and made the city the center of Mississippi protests and voter registration struggles. I was teaching approximately thirty miles away from Greenwood and that made it quite difficult for me to participate in a majority of the marches which were held in the mornings. But when there was a march at night or on weekends I was in attendance. Activist leaders scheduled a march in downtown Greenwood in support of voter registration, and police dogs were put on black people who were attempting to register. The march was led by a Methodist minister, the Reverend Donald Tucker. The police came on the scene and denounced Reverend Tucker as a "son of a bitch" and claimed that John Kennedy was his "God." At the time the Kennedy family was very popular among black people. Reverend Tucker's dog bites were so severe that he had to be hospitalized and that caused a huge uproar in Mississippi. The attack against him received national news coverage and it even brought comedian activist Dick Gregory to

Greenwood to participate in the marches. One of the most prominent Mississippi civil rights leaders was Fannie Lou Hamer, who also came to Greenwood to assist in the movement.

During this period, hundreds were arrested because of their nonviolent protests, and civil rights activists were subjected to repeated violence. The discrimination was obvious and blatant, designed to keep blacks from passing the voter registration test. Black applicants were asked ridiculous questions such as how many bubbles were there in a bar of soap or difficult questions concerning the provisions in the state constitution. If black persons attempted to vote, their names were printed in the local newspaper. The next day they would be fired from their job. If there was even a rumor that blacks were thinking about exercising their right to vote, they would be terminated. The news of the difficulties in Leflore County quickly spread and representatives from various national civil rights organizations came to the Delta to assist. There was a two-story building on Broad Street where the strategy meetings were held. Some of the more violent-prone white people began to shoot into the building quite frequently when they knew that blacks were meeting. There were other offices associated with the movement that had already been burned down to the ground.

Mechanization had also come to the Greenwood area about this time and it downgraded the role of manual labor in the cotton business. The time when blacks were picked up in large numbers from Greenwood and transported in trucks to pick cotton to make a few dollars was rapidly ending. The plantation owners no longer needed a vast cadre of black laborers because of the mechanical cotton pickers and this loss of jobs left many blacks, as poor as they already were, even worse off. Many of them nearly starved to death.

A group called the Student Nonviolent Coordinating Committee (SNCC) arrived in Greenwood about this time. They were sent to attempt to register black people to vote because the black vote was the only way governmental policies and poor economic conditions were going to improve. The men who headed the movement in Greenwood included Sam Block, Willie Peacock, and Lawrence Guyot.

Also very visible was a brave young SNCC organizer named Bob Moses. Moses was responsible for coordinating local movements in different towns throughout the state of Mississippi.

I became involved with SNCC by attending meetings and participating in boycotts and marches. My involvement in the movement occasionally put me close to the dangers that many of the more prominent activist-leaders were frequently subjected to. There were many incidents happening during this time. I recall that late one Sunday evening one of two SNCC offices was burned down. A fellow teacher from Gentry High School who had been visiting my family went there with me. After I finished assisting Sam Block in cleaning the office, my friend and I left and headed in the direction of my home, shortly thereafter to learn that the second SNCC office had been firebombed.

There was another incident that I recall. One Saturday night around 11:30 p.m., a carload of white men wearing dark glasses circled the two-story SNCC office building located on Avenue I Street. The SNCC workers Sam Block, Willie Peacock, and Lawrence Guyot spotted them from the second floor and were forced to jump out the window to escape. They ran hastily down the alley until they reached my home. They banged on the door in a desperate state until I finally opened it. They were out of breath as they informed me that the Klan was chasing them. It was certainly an unsettling event for me, knowing that my two children were sleeping soundly in their bed unaware of any potential dangers. Chris went to retrieve some water for the exhausted men and it helped to calm them down. With the house lights off and the streetlight shining through the window, I could see how to dial Bob Moses, who was in Greenville. He drove to my home and picked them up. These were just a few incidents that come to mind as I reflect on my involvement in the movement.

I also remember Medgar Evers, who was heavily involved in the civil rights movement. Evers was a native of Mississippi and seemingly fearless as an activist. He was another great African American whose life ended violently and tragically. It was June 12, 1963, and President John F. Kennedy's speech supporting civil rights had been televised that day. It was only a few hours afterwards that Evers was ambushed, struck in the back by a bullet from a rifle as he was getting out of his parked car in his home carport. He just so happened to be carrying a box full of NAACP shirts as he stumbled to his death. I heard of his murder the next morning at work. Walking out of the cafeteria I had spotted a group of principals huddled together. My principal walked up to me and said, "You know they got Evers last night." I remember how badly the news hurt me. I recalled that a month before his death he was in Greenwood where he delivered a powerful speech. He had emphatically stated, "I'm going to do the same thing in Jackson that you all are doing in Greenwood. We are going to win this fight for equality and freedom!" I called Chris on the phone to break the sad news to her, but she already knew and was watching the breaking story on the television news.

Evers was mourned all over the world, accounts of his life filled with recognition for his contributions in fighting for African American equality. Just a few days after Evers's death a man by the name of Byron De La Beckwith was accused of the assassination. It seemed that I was affected by Evers's death even more because I knew the accused assassin. I often watched De La Beckwith shooting dice at the store where I worked as a young man. I couldn't imagine anyone from Greenwood responsible for murdering one of the greatest civil rights leaders in Mississippi. It appeared that when it came to avenging Medgar's death, another white man was going to get away with the cold-blooded murder of a black person.

A few weeks after this terrible event happened I had to go through a recertification process to continue teaching. Black educators needing to meet the state recertification requirement could not do so at the all-white University of Mississippi; we were given the choice to go to Atlanta University or Tuskegee Institute in Alabama. I chose to go to Tuskegee while Chris was still a student at Mississippi Valley State College.

When I finished the course work at Tuskegee, I was in search of a job until school started. I was still teaching in the system where the school session was split, which meant that I was unable to teach until

October, so I needed work for a few months to provide for my family. I was finally able to obtain employment at the Cotton Compress. I remember one particular day when all the employees were on break. Most of the black workers knew that I was a teacher; they would call me "Fess," short for professor. There was one guy who could neither read nor write and he had worked a considerable amount of overtime that week. He wanted me to calculate the amount of pay that he should receive at the end of the week. I obliged his request, but a foreman overheard our conversation and I was fired on the spot. I had no idea how I was going to make ends meet now. The next morning I went to the unemployment office and found out that the Baldwin Piano Company in Greenwood was hiring.

I was able to obtain employment in the staining department at the Baldwin plant. I was responsible for scraping the furniture before it was sent to an experienced worker for staining. The supervisor was pleased with my work, but I couldn't let him know that I was a teacher or I would have been fired immediately. The supervisor eventually told me that he wanted to give me full-time permanent work. I didn't want a full-time position because I was returning to teaching in October. I tried to avoid going to the office to respond to the full-time offer, but the job offer was made two weeks before I was due to return to teaching. The plant manager was someone with whom I was acquainted; he sold insurance in the black community, his clientele being primarily those who couldn't really afford insurance. I was one of the blacks who couldn't afford insurance at the time myself. He explained to me that he was having trouble with some of the boys who were employees in the plant. He then asked me if I could work around white women. I was very offended by the question and I immediately said, "Hell, I don't need this job! I'm a teacher!" I was terminated by the end of the week. I still had one more week before I was scheduled to teach, so I had to borrow money from a loan shark at a high interest rate in order to make it to the next month. I was quite ready when school started in October because the last few months had definitely been a roller-coaster ride for me in a number of ways.

A month or so after I got settled into work, another great leader was assassinated in Dallas, Texas. It was November 22, 1963, a few days before Thanksgiving, when President John F. Kennedy was killed. I remember that all the teachers left the classrooms and gathered in the hallway to console one another. The principal showed no emotion and told us that if we wanted our jobs we had better get back to teaching! African Americans loved the Kennedy family and their style. I was personally just impressed with how they handled their business and I was devastated over the fact that someone had killed him. It was shocking to me because I never thought I would live in an era when a president would suffer assassination. President Kennedy was shot while he rode in the presidential car alongside his wife. It seemed that anyone who supported the movement for black equal rights was severely punished. Among many southern whites, apparently the Kennedys were hated as much as blacks were. There were many motorists who had bumper stickers that read "KKK," which stood for "Knock out the Kennedys and King!" I was paying close attention to everything that was transpiring and I was becoming more and more interested in how far blacks were willing to go to attain equality.

Chris and I were doing pretty well during this time and our family was happy, but this blissful status didn't last long. I had been getting checked periodically ever since Chris contracted tuberculosis and I always came out okay. In my most recent examination when my X-rays came back the doctor explained to me that I had a shadow on my right lung. They assured me that they would keep an eye on it and I went on with my daily routine. One day I was in my classroom coughing so continuously that I was forced to walk out. When I made it to the washroom, I spit into the toilet bowl and realized that I was coughing up blood, though not enough to get me too alarmed. I walked back inside the classroom and continued teaching. I came home and told Chris what transpired and she insisted that I go and see Dr. Fred Sandifer. He ran some tests and had me go to the health department to take additional X-rays. The next morning I went back to work. Each time I coughed I would get a dull pain on the right side of my back and now I was starting to get concerned. And I had real cause. It was about two or three o'clock in the morning when I began hemorrhaging quite a bit. Chris was forced to call my brother Andrew, who came over and took me to Greenwood Leflore Hospital. She was pregnant, expecting our fourth child, and this was not the time to be faced with health challenges from me! I prayed on the way to the hospital that this was not a serious enough health condition that I would be required to be away from my family. I was solely responsible for taking care of the household with Chris attending school. A health scare was definitely something that I wasn't prepared for, but on the ride to the hospital I began to mentally prepare for the worst!

The Depths
of My Struggle

It was February of 1964 when I was admitted to Greenwood Leflore Hospital. The test results showed that I had contracted tuberculosis. I was quarantined while at the hospital for three or four days before I was allowed to come home. The children weren't allowed to be around me, but they tried to peek in on me whenever they got an opportunity. I remember that "The Twist" by Chubby Checker was popular during that time and my son Donald loved doing that dance. He was around three years old and he would stand at the doorway and say, "Daddy, do you want me to do the twist?" I would muster a smile through all my discomfort because I knew this was his way of trying to cheer me up; he knew that I wasn't myself. Our fourth child was due any day now and the doctor had already informed me that I would have to be out of the house before the baby was born. I stayed around the house for another two weeks and during that time my principal, Mr. Brown, brought me my check. I had spent so much time away from work due to my illness that my check was only a couple of hundred dollars. More disturbing, Mr. Brown informed me that the school could not hold my job for me. It was only February and school wouldn't be out until May, which was too much time to have a substitute teacher in my position.

A week later, around February 20, Andrew drove me to the state hospital. I was admitted to the sanatorium in Magee, Mississippi, where Chris had been a patient a few years earlier. I wanted to know how long I was going to be hospitalized, but initially the doctor who admitted me had no time frame in mind. When he was able to take a closer look at my X-rays he gave me up to six months to be hospitalized. I was extremely disappointed to hear this news because I didn't want to be away from home that long. After I got checked in, they immediately began administering treatments. I dreaded eating the food because it had absolutely no appealing taste to it. But clearly there were more serious issues to contend with. The spot on my right lung necessitated an operation, something I didn't look forward to, though it was completed without complications. There were a lot of pills required to treat tuberculosis during that time and I was required to take about ten pills at a time, three times a day. My only consolation for this agonizing routine was the realization that the pills would help me get completely well. The patients were allowed to go to the lobby at certain times of the day. It was usually an hour in the morning and an hour in the evening. The other times we were confined to our rooms. I went to the library and checked out numerous books. I read every day because I had never before had this much free time on my hands.

A week after my quarantine began, my fourth child was born, Darryl Jordan. I was extremely disappointed that I wasn't there to welcome my third son into the world, but I knew that he would be very well taken care of during my absence. I was trying to adjust to being away, but being sick and bored was not a great combination. A lady from the rehabilitation office finally approached me and said they had checked with the physicians about my being able to teach while confined to the facility. They had looked at my record and found out that I had a degree in science. There were about nine students who, unfortunately, had to leave high school because of the disease. I eventually began teaching those students twice a day, an hour in the morning and an hour in the afternoon. It took away from the monotony and the depression of having to be confined. I continued that routine for the next few months and the time passed more quickly because of it.

On August 24, I received some more heartbreaking news. My mother had lost her fight with diabetes and she had passed earlier that day. Momma worked hard all her life, but she neglected her health and it finally took its toll. She never did eat well and she made sweets and dry foods her regular diet. At the time that Momma was a diabetic there was no effective treatment for the disease except for insulin shots. I can remember many times giving Momma her shot. There were numerous times that she didn't have the money for insulin and she would just go without it. Momma had a strong will and a desire to keep working and we never knew how badly the disease was affecting her. It wasn't until she developed cataracts and could not see well that it became obvious she was sicker than we thought. I received a furlough from the hospital in order to go home for the funeral. When I arrived in Greenwood, I was advised not to attend the service because of the contagious disease that I was recuperating from. Although I did not attend the funeral service, I was able to view the body at the funeral home to say my goodbyes to Momma. It was very painful to say goodbye to the woman who had given me life. The day of the funeral I stayed home and reflected on all the good and bad times that I experienced growing up. I thought about all the love and support that Momma had given us throughout the years. The tears began to stream down my face now that Momma was gone. My consolation was that I knew she was in a better place, and I was so thankful to have had such a strong dedicated woman as my mother.

While I was on furlough, I ran into a man who was a principal. His name was Howard Austin and he was looking for a science teacher. He informed me that he had a job for me once I was released from the hospital. A week or so after I made it back to the state hospital it was time for me to have another checkup. The doctor walked up to me and said, "David, you are being discharged and now you can really go back to teaching." I called Chris with the good news and she rode down with one of her cousins to pick me up. I was happy to be going home, but there were some loose ends that needed to be tied up before my family's life could return to normalcy. Chris had been unable to attend school while I was sick because she stayed home with the children. She also didn't have transportation during that time because our car had been repossessed. The situation had gotten so bad that Chris had to go on welfare for about three months while I was away. My children couldn't even receive free lunches because the principal stated that I was a teacher and I should have saved my money for a rainy day. That meant Joyce and David Jr. were forced to take bag lunches to school. The one thing I knew when I got home was that I needed to get my hands on some money.

The job that I had been offered was quite a distance away. It was 120 miles round trip, which meant I definitely had to get my hands on a dependable vehicle. I ended up borrowing six hundred dollars from the credit union and half of that went to get my car back. The credit union wasn't worried about my being able to repay the loan because the officials knew about the job that I had lined up. I was hitchhiking to Jackson, Mississippi, to pick up my vehicle when a minister pulled up and took me to my destination. I got my vehicle and headed home. I knew it was time for me to begin to put the pieces of my life back together.

I began teaching science in Humphreys County at Louise High School in the fall of 1964. I was rather excited about the change of schools, but not too enthusiastic about the distance getting to and from work. I allowed the band teacher to ride with me and share in the gas expense. There were approximately three hundred students attending the school and they were pretty well-disciplined. The principal, Mr. Austin, was a graduate of Mississippi Vocational College (now Mississippi Valley State University) and I was extremely grateful that he had given me this opportunity. The school had a football team, but it wasn't very good. I commuted every day, but sometimes I had to stay overnight to complete the extra duties assigned to the teachers. If I was required to stay over, I would rent a room from Mr. Austin's father. I remember the first check that I received; the amount was $382. I had to excuse myself from the class because I felt myself becoming quite emotional as I stared at the paycheck in my hand. I strolled down the hallway and went into a room where we kept all of our chemicals, and I broke down in tears. It was a lot of money to have during those times and I was so grateful for having a job that paid a decent salary. I had been through so much and

I hadn't seen that much money in quite some time. I was so overwhelmed that I had a difficult time finishing up the remainder of the day. I really wanted to leave once my paycheck was in my hand, but I had an obligation to complete the school day.

I got home and the three children ran up to the car like they always did. Chris came out with Darryl in her arms and noticed that I was overjoyed about something. I told the children to get ready because we were going out to have hamburgers. It had been a long time since we had been able to enjoy a family outing. A few weeks later I purchased a television, which made everyone in the house extremely happy.

I was back on my feet again and feeling pretty good about life, but it wasn't long before another minor setback occurred. I was on my way to work one morning and the heavy fog made driving conditions quite hazardous. I approached five or six cars piled up and I was unable to stop in time. I ran into the back of a truck and wrecked the front end of my car. I suffered a bloody nose and the passenger riding with me got a blister on his head. I was sitting in the driver's seat thinking to myself, no, not another catastrophe. I had a wrecked vehicle and I also had to call in to be off from work. I took the car to be fixed and by the grace of God the man gave me a loaner car to drive at no charge while my car was being repaired. I hopped in the car and headed to the doctor's office to make certain that I hadn't suffered any internal injuries.

The year 1964 ended with another black man's violent death. It was a chilly December night and I had to stay overnight in Louise. I received the news that Sam Cooke had been killed at the age of thirty-three. It immediately saddened me because I was a huge fan of his music. It was very disturbing to me that all the people whom I admired were being killed. I was tired of the violent deaths that were occurring way too often and I couldn't help but wonder when the turmoil was going to end. There were a lot of things that were happening in my life that could be deemed distressing events. However, I believed that the many struggles that I faced were only making me a stronger man and preparing me to be a leader.

In the spring of 1965, I found out that I was eligible to receive a scholarship, the National Science Foundation Scholarship for science teachers. I had applied to several universities to receive one of the scholarships. I had Chris check my mail each day while I was at school because I was waiting on a reply from one of the colleges, hoping to receive a scholarship to further my education. I came home from work one day and finally there was a big envelope from Dillard University in New Orleans. I could feel my stomach fluttering as I slowly opened the letter. My eyes got extremely big when I spotted the first line. It read, "We are pleased to inform you that you have been accepted in the Science Program at Dillard University." The program was starting in June and it lasted for eight weeks. The whole family gathered around cheering over my good news. I couldn't begin to express how happy we all were. This was a major breakthrough for me, to be able to continue my education, which would also increase my earning potential. We knew that we had money coming for the summer so I treated my family to something that could enhance all of our lives: I bought an air conditioner to deal with the Delta heat.

I packed up my vehicle and started toward my destination in Louisiana. I had never been to New Orleans and it immediately showed when I arrived in the city. I was by no means familiar with the area and I ended up getting on Rampart Street headed in the wrong direction. I could hear a group of foreigners shouting, "Stop that man! He's going the wrong way!" I was lucky that I didn't get killed and I quickly turned around and headed in the right direction. I still didn't know where I was going, but I ran into a soldier and asked him where Dillard University was located. I was extremely desperate to find it, so I offered him two dollars to drive me to the school in my car. When I pulled up to the campus parking lot, a light indicating that something was wrong with the vehicle was flashing. I discovered that I needed another alternator, an expense I was unprepared for, so I just left the car sitting in the lot for eight weeks. It was a really good experience to attend Dillard University and I was pleased that I had been given the opportunity to study there.

It was time to start the fall semester again and I began dreading having to travel the long commute to and from work. I was a highly qualified teacher and I was disappointed that I had to go so far from my hometown in order to teach. I had applied to get into the Greenwood school system, but officials wouldn't hire me. I was a Jordan and to a lot of people that name was heavily connected to the civil rights movement. My brother Andrew was the head of the local NAACP in Greenwood and Poppa was still active in the movement. The principals in the area were told not to hire any member of the Jordan family. My married sister had a different last name, which meant she didn't have to contend with the stigma associated with the Jordan name. The black principals were good people for the most part, but they were cautious. They didn't want to be involved with anyone who was a part of the movement and thereby jeopardize their own position.

There was a time when Andrew was teaching, but once it was known about his involvement in the movement he was fired. It was common practice that if employers found out about any black person's affiliation with the movement he or she would be automatically terminated. Andrew began to struggle because he had no job and no one was willing to hire him. He eventually packed up and went to Toledo, Ohio. My oldest brother, Clevester, who lived there, persuaded him to make the move. He was certain that Andrew could get a teaching job and it happened just as Clevester predicted. Andrew got a teaching job and was able to make Toledo his permanent new home.

The Voting Rights Act was passed in August of 1965 during President Lyndon Johnson's administration. It outlawed the discriminatory practices adopted in many southern states, including the literacy test and poll taxes as prerequisites to voting. Dr. King and other prominent blacks involved in the voting rights struggle were in Washington, D.C., to observe the bill signing. President Johnson stated that every American citizen must have an equal right to vote.

The Greenwood Voters' League was also established in 1965. The new organization totaled about forty people who voted in Leflore

County and Greenwood. The body needed a president and it elected me. I was the youngest in the founding group and I was so impressionable that I readily accepted the position. I reorganized the group and gave it the official name, the Greenwood Voters' League. There was a prestigious group of people representing the Voters' League, such people as Rev. J. D. Collins, who had a shoe repairing business in Greenwood, Edward Cochran, who ran a hotel, and Mr. Lewis Golden, who was a well-known local barber. These people wanted to see a change for blacks in Leflore County and they believed that I was the man to lead the organization. I was pleased with the way things were going with my new position, but I had to continue to go away to school in order to advance my professional career. Mr. Golden was the vice president of the organization and he ably filled in for me until I could provide a more direct and involved leadership role in the president's position.

The following fall I decided that I would not return to Louise High School. I felt the 120-mile round trip was too long a drive and it seemed that a lot of my paycheck was being used to get back and forth to work. The Greenwood school district was still adamant about not allowing me an opportunity to teach in the system. I went to Carroll County to see the principal, Mr. Irvin Whittaker, and he informed me that his science teacher was leaving for graduate school. He said that he would have no problem hiring me for the vacant position. I immediately told him that I wouldn't be available for duty on the first day because of a prior commitment. Mr. Whittaker let me know that it wouldn't be a problem and I accepted the job. I was going to be a science teacher at Marshall High School in Carrollton, only fifteen miles from Greenwood, which was much better than the great distance that I had been traveling. I was often so exhausted from driving back and forth to Louise that it limited my time with my family. I was more than ready and willing to accept both of my new challenges. I couldn't wait to start my new teaching position and I was ready to take on the responsibility of being the president of the Greenwood Voters' League!

A Salute to the Sixties

In 1966, I received an opportunity to attend Kansas State College
of Pittsburg to work toward my graduate degree. There were approximately sixty students from across the country enrolled in
the college's Science Institute. I was studying chemistry and I needed
to complete all graduate classes in order to renew my teaching cer-
tification. The usual procedure was to receive a check for half of the
money due me after class registration. It didn't matter what school
I had attended; this had always been the policy. This time when I
registered, however, there was no money available. A big tornado in
Kansas had recently occurred and the town bank had blown away.
It was hard to imagine such a thing, and if I hadn't witnessed the
destruction with my own eyes, I probably wouldn't have believed it.
I was unable to send money home to Chris despite her need and ex-
pectation for that first installment check. The money was for Chris
to pay bills and to get groceries to last a couple of months until I returned home. I usually sent about three or four hundred dollars, but
this time I had nothing to send. Eventually I had to call my old job
and ask one of the guys to extend my wife credit until the problem
was resolved. He assured me that it wouldn't be a problem. I had
Chris gather the kids and drive to the store to get the items that she
needed. I made sure I paid off that debt as soon as I obtained revenue. I was then able to concentrate on why I was away in the first
place. I continued to stay focused on my studies as the summer days
dwindled away.

I was ready to return home, although I loved the idea of being able
to experience new things and different challenges. My feelings were

completely demolished a week before school was scheduled to end. I was told that I couldn't get the graduate credits for my eight hours of chemistry because the University of Mississippi didn't accept students from Mississippi Valley State College. The Kansas State staff felt that if my own state wouldn't accept me in their graduate school then Kansas State wasn't going to allow me in their program either. All the long nights of studying and being away from my family for the whole summer appeared to be in vain. I was stunned by what I was told, but I refused to believe that I had wasted my time and that all my hard work was about to go down the drain.

I couldn't sleep the night after receiving that awful news; I tossed and turned most of the night until I had no choice but to call Chris. She was my voice of reason, even when I couldn't see the brightest picture. I had received some gloomy news and I had no idea about what to expect, but I knew she would give me the strength to deal with any and all obstacles thrown in my path. She would also comfort me by reassuring me that this was only a temporary setback. The next morning I was working in the lab and one of the professors pulled me to the back of the class. He said the dean of the graduate school had informed him that if I acquired all Bs as my grades, I would receive graduate credit like everyone else. This was definitely great news and my prayers had been answered. I made two Bs and received my graduate credits just as I was promised. My mission had been accomplished and now it was time for me to return home.

In October of 1966 Poppa suffered a stroke and was hospitalized in the Greenwood Leflore Hospital. Poppa didn't eat right and after Momma passed he completely neglected his diet. He never ate any vegetables and his health definitely suffered as a result. His illness was very hard to explain to the children because they adored their grandfather. He would come by to watch the news on our television a lot of evenings and this allowed the children an opportunity to bond with him. I remember visiting Poppa at the hospital and being called a nigger for absolutely no reason. I was only inquiring about the condition of my father. I guess the nurse became annoyed with my ability to ask intelligent questions. It was common back then for white folks to think that blacks thought they were smarter if they had an education or a job with authority.

Poppa stayed in the hospital approximately a month, but on November 20, 1966, he made his transition from this life. He was now with the woman whom he had shared the majority of his life with and who was the mother of his five children. I was able to attend Poppa's funeral, unlike when sickness kept me from being present at my mother's services. I was saying goodbye to a man who had definitely been a fine example of manhood. I was delighted that Poppa had an opportunity to see me heading in the right direction of making something distinctive out of my life. I was the youngest of his five children, but I was determined at all cost to contribute positively in carrying the Jordan name forward. Poppa's hard work for blacks to have justice and equality would definitely not go in vain. He was buried now and I knew that he would want me to stay on track in making him and Momma proud. I didn't have much time to grieve before I got back to business.

My brother Will Henry was the only one left in the house where he and Poppa lived. He was still pretty much a loner; his company primarily consisted of a bunch of dogs trailing behind him. There were many people who thought that he was extremely strange and some even called him the "dog man," but no one bothered him. He loved his dogs and they loved him back and the fact that he preferred their company over humans, that they were his constant companions, even living inside the house with him, made him a bit eccentric, but nothing more.

In 1967 Chris joined me at Marshall High School to complete her student teaching. Her college professors and the dean felt that with my teaching proficiency and experience she should be placed under my guidance and supervision. They didn't usually allow married couples to work together, but my advisor, Mr. John A. James, and the college dean made an exception this time. I was teaching chemistry, biology, and I believe one other science class; Chris would be teaching biology.

During this time, desegregation was just coming to the South. It was not a shock that black students were deficient in their education because they had not been exposed to the changes in science education that were rapidly occurring. The federal government finally began placing new education material into the black schools, but the pace was never ideal. I had been to graduate schools, although I had not yet earned my master's degree. I had seen some of the up-to-date science materials that were now being used in the classroom and I had acquired a better understanding of the latest technology in science. When I taught in a small school, however, I wasn't able to perform demonstrations and experiments, though things were now improving. Black education was making some progress as the benefit of school integration was starting to make a difference in some schools. Two of my children, David Jr. and Joyce, were among the six students who integrated the schools in Greenwood. There were films and books showing up to help advance the black students. At my school I was the only science instructor teaching high school science and I had more than enough materials to take my teaching to another level.

When Chris received her degree in science, they offered her a job at the school. We were now working together and I was delighted about it. It improved our professional and working situation and made our close marital relationship even closer. At night, once we got the children settled, we would look over materials together. We graded papers and bounced ideas off each other. The next morning, we would get up and drive our fifteen-mile trip to work; being together like this I considered a glorious time for our union.

In the summer of 1967 I attended the University of Wyoming. It seemed like I travelled back in time as I made the three-day journey to get to my destination. The old wagon wheels that I saw along the way and the comical little country towns with their rustic physical structures and visible artifacts reminded me of old Western movies, a genre of which I was a huge fan. On the journey, I ate for the first time in my life a meal that included bear meat. When we arrived in the state of Colorado I saw the Rocky Mountains covered in deep snow. The temperature had dropped drastically and I remember wondering if the bus was going to even make it up the steep hills. We made it into the town where the university was located and though I had no idea of what to expect, I wasn't afraid to embrace new experiences. It had been a long three-day trip but after we arrived, I was able to get settled pretty quickly.

I had a roommate who was a Mormon from Utah. He wanted to know all about the South and for the most part we got along just fine. There was an African American man from Milwaukee and an African American woman from Miami, so including me there was a total of three blacks in the institute's degree program. I was extremely proud that I was in the program because to me it meant that I was only a few steps away from achieving another milestone. Dr. Hardin was the man who headed the institute. I was enrolled in organic chemistry and the instructors who taught the course covered the subject matter at a rapid pace. The course was really advanced for me and I had to do my best to keep up. The information was abundant and to the point; four blackboards in the classroom were in constant use in the instructional process. The formulas were extremely difficult and I had to scribble my notes rapidly, sometimes illegibly, in order not to fall behind. Clearly the instruction went far beyond simple textbook knowledge, so I burned a lot of midnight oil just to keep up with the fast pace. I was the only African American male from the South in the program and I was especially conscious of nonsoutherners' opinions of black southerners' intellect, so I deliberately refrained from asking questions. Nevertheless, I continued to apply myself and to add more graduate courses in my pursuit of receiving a degree.

In February of 1968, Chris and I purchased our own home. My old music teacher and her husband previously owned the house. She was the teacher who played the song that I wrote for Chris during our high school courtship. She and her husband had retired from the school system and felt it was time to move on. We were fortunate to have found the house in the first place. We were driving around town on a family outing, my intent largely being to show my children where I once lived and to shed some history on my humble beginnings. I wanted them to see the plantations where I once picked cotton and to see that things were not always easy for their parents growing up. We just lucked up on seeing the "for sale" sign. We stopped the car and inquired about the property. It was a modest house but certainly adequate for my family's needs. We immediately retained an attorney and refinanced the house. We were doing well with two salaries and we were extremely happy in our marriage and family life. Now we had a house that we were purchasing and we had a 1966 Chevy parked out front. However, I had come to accept that during this time of my life things could happen in the blink of an eye that could destroy your joy. Still, we remained optimistic that the course our life was on would not be interrupted by anything disruptive.

It was two months after purchasing our home that the African American race suffered a devastating loss. On April 4, 1968, Dr. Martin Luther King Jr., one of the most prominent leaders in African American history, was assassinated. I remember that evening quite well, although it is not a fond memory. Chris and I had worked that day and we were at home winding down. I could hear the kids watching television in the kitchen and I went to check to make sure they hadn't neglected their studies. The telephone rang, causing me to halt dead in my tracks. I answered it and on the other end was Mrs. Jackson. She was the nurse who had treated me when I had the fender bender a few years prior. She was also quite aware, based on our conversations, that I was involved in the civil rights struggle in Leflore County. Mrs. Jackson finally shared with me the heartbreaking news that Dr. King had been shot in Memphis, Tennessee. I was astounded and I quickly rushed to tell Chris the news. We immediately turned on the television and saw national news commentator Sam Donaldson in tears. There was nothing that we could do but break down crying ourselves because we were completely devastated. All the national correspondents were broadcasting about this terrible tragedy. Dr. King had been standing on the second-floor balcony of the Lorraine Motel when he was felled by a single rifle bullet. He was rushed to the hospital, but unfortunately the medical staff was unable to save his life. The black community was outraged all over the country and showed their anger during the outbreak of numerous urban riots. The blacks in Greenwood attacked the stores in the city. They burned down one of the Chinese grocery stores and scared the local Chinese population badly. City officials immediately met with the black leaders to urge peace because they didn't know what to expect next. Senator Robert Kennedy, on the campaign trail stumping for votes in the Democratic presidential primary, made a passionate speech about King's death. It was addressed to the country, but was especially directed at the national black community to salve their emotional despair and to quell retaliatory violence. With great compassion he let black people know that he understood their pain for he too had lost someone close to him, his brother, to violence. Kennedy knew personal tragedy and his heart went out to the nation and to the King family for what they were now suffering.

The governor of Georgia, Jimmy Carter, accompanied Mrs. King to Memphis to pick up Dr. King's body. It helped ease the pain just a little to see that Kennedy and Carter sympathized with the black race. They were well aware that we had lost an outstanding leader and, to many, a great friend. Dr. King was thirty-nine years old when his life violently ended. He was only a few years older than I was and he had left four children behind. I thought about how difficult it was going to be for Mrs. King to raise four children alone and I sympathized with her. I couldn't imagine the pressure that would be placed on Chris if I was no longer around to help raise our family. I admired Mrs. King's courage and her strength for being supportive in her husband's fight for racial justice. Dr. King was a man of powerful words and many of his often-quoted lines came to my mind as I reflected on him in life and in death. One quote that continually resonates with me, even today, because it's helped inspire me in my own struggles to uplift my people are the words "If a man hadn't discovered something that he will die for, he isn't fit to live!"

The world had not quite recovered from the death of King before another tragedy occurred. This time it was Senator Robert Kennedy who was himself a victim of senseless violence. It was June 5, 1968, and he had just won the California primary election for the Democratic nomination for president. The thought of another Kennedy running the country posed a threat for some and great optimism and encouragement for the African American. Unfortunately he was shot as he walked through the kitchen of the Ambassador Hotel in Los Angeles. I had the same admiration for Robert Kennedy as I did for his brother. I felt this was another devastating loss for the nation and especially for black Americans.

My whole family accompanied me when it was time for me to return to Wyoming for the summer. I didn't want to be away from them because enough tragic events had occurred that made me realize just how precious each second counted with loved ones. I needed them close by as I dealt emotionally with the painful tragedies that had occurred in the last few months. It was tough on me to see the faces of all those white people in Wyoming, knowing that many still had no respect for a black man's life. But many of them embraced me like never before and I was elated to see that I was now being respected. I didn't know or care what was behind the equal treatment, so I just welcomed it because I knew this was how things were supposed to be. Chris had also received a scholarship to the University of Wyoming. She was not in the graduate degree component of the program, but she was taking some advanced classes and the additional knowledge would move her teaching to a higher level. The kids were having a great time, playing ball and participating in other activities that children enjoy. The summer went by pretty quickly and I was getting closer to reaching my final goal. It was common practice that everyone who went to college got a sticker for their car displaying the name of their school. I enjoyed placing my sticker on the back window of my car and representing the University of Wyoming. I thought it was rather unique to be attending school there because no one in Greenwood, Mississippi, that I knew had gone there before me.

It was time for the school year to begin and both Chris and I were still teaching at Marshall High School. There was a troubling but delicate incident we had to handle a couple of weeks after school had been in session. One day we arrived home from school and Joyce met us at the car. She said, "Daddy, I got into a fight today. A white boy knocked my books out of my hand and started pushing me." Joyce went on to inform us that she was forced to defend herself. It resulted in both students going to the office to face the principal. I couldn't imagine a boy fighting a girl and I definitely couldn't accept someone putting their hands on my daughter. Joyce had always been a well-behaved student at school because she was a smart little girl who was focused on her schoolwork. She could read early and was quite eager to learn as much as she could. Teachers were always informing us how much they enjoyed having Joyce in their classroom. It was hard imagining her being involved in any inappropriate behavior. The superintendent, Dr. Dribben, would always tell us how nice our children were and his wife was also Joyce's teacher. I immediately asked my daughter how the principal had resolved the issue. Joyce informed us that the principal was firm on punishing only her because the boy claimed she had started the whole ordeal. I was livid after hearing this and I told Chris to get back in the car because we were going to confront the principal. It was one thing to have to suffer occasional verbal attacks by being called a "nigger," but there was no way that I was going to allow my children to start suffering any physical attacks. I could immediately detect a very evasive attitude as soon as we sat across from the principal. The way he responded to our questions was definitely not to our satisfaction. We quickly discovered that talking to the principal was a waste of time, so we left.

The next day we went to pay Dr. Dribben a visit to try and get some results. I explained to him what Joyce had shared with us concerning the incident at school. He knew that the Jordan children were well-behaved and would avoid trouble. I went on to tell him that we were not satisfied with the results that we received when we spoke with the principal. I looked him dead in the eye and said, "Dr. Dribben, if you can't straighten this out then I will see if the Justice Department can't step in because under court order my child, and every other black student, has the right to be there!" He quickly responded with a nervous chuckle and said, "David Jordan, we don't have to go that far!" We left and I felt confident that this problem would quickly be resolved. I wanted him to understand that I would protect my children by any means necessary. They would not be the victims of any malicious behavior while trying to obtain an education. However, Dr. Dribben talked with the teachers and resolved the problem.

In November of that same year I buried another family member. My brother Clevester passed away from diabetes. He was still residing in Toledo, Ohio, and I left for his funeral right before Thanksgiving. Andrew picked me up at the bus station and I got an opportunity to spend quality time with him. I had said goodbye to Momma and Poppa, and now I was burying my eldest brother; all three of them would be greatly missed.

In 1969, Chris obtained a job in the Greenwood school district, but I still wasn't allowed to teach in Greenwood. Chris had inquired several times to the superintendent regarding employment and he finally hired her. He informed her that he had a job for her as a team teacher, which meant two teachers, in this case one black and one white, would be in the classroom. It was during the integration process and they definitely didn't want to trust a black teacher managing a classroom alone that contained white students. Still, with her hiring, Chris had broken through a barrier, even though the new situation was not ideal. If for no other reason, however, the pay scale made the irregular teaching arrangement more palatable. The Greenwood district paid a thousand dollars more than the county school system, which was considered a good salary for someone only holding a bachelor's degree. It appeared that it was certainly going to be an interesting experience for Chris.

My last and final summer at the University of Wyoming was an experience that I would never forget. I had become friends with a man we called "Big Jim" because he weighed about three hundred pounds. He was a nice guy and he also had a vehicle on campus for him and his friends to move around in. The small group of us who "hung out" together would occasionally pay for someone to cook us some ham hocks, neck bones, cornbread, and greens. After we ate on Saturday night, we would then go to the local bar for a cold beer. I remember thinking the drinking spot was so peculiar because there were peanut shells all over the floor, almost up to the patrons' ankles. I would watch with amazement the dances that they were performing because I couldn't do the two-step or square dance. Big Jim and I did buy us some western hats and we would go downtown and proudly walk around wearing them and have such a great time in the experience. I still missed my family and nothing ever filled the void of not having them around me. I remember how I would call home and the children would take turns asking for the phone just to hear my voice. They always asked the same question and that was when I was coming home. I was gone for only ten weeks, but being away from them for more than a day was definitely something to contend with. We were a tight-knit family; Chris and I loved the children dearly and they were aware of it.

I was fulfilling the requirements that would allow me to return to Greenwood with a master's degree. I completed my thesis and then it was time for me to go before three professors and get quizzed on what I knew about the walk on the moon. I answered the questions proficiently in the beginning, but the questions became more difficult and I no longer could give the right responses. I could only hope that my anxiety wasn't too obvious, but my heart felt like it had dropped to the floor as I glanced at the faces of the three professors. They dismissed me and told me to wait outside while the three of them made a decision on my fate. I was under a tremendous amount of pressure because there was no way that I wanted to return home without completing my mission. It was about ten minutes later that one of the professors came out and said, "Mr. Jordan, congratulations, you passed everything!" I felt as light as a feather and I could have easily floated right out of there. This was great news and I couldn't wait to share it with Chris.

I had only one other obligation to fulfill and that was the residency requirement. This necessitated that I remain on campus until graduation, which was ten more days. I called Chris and she was ecstatic to hear all the good news. She then reminded me that we needed to drive to Jacksonville, Florida, to pick up our son Darryl. Chris's mother had relocated to Florida to be with her son. She sold her house and furniture and moved to Florida to relax and enjoy the sun. Occasionally she came back to Mississippi to visit and usually she took one of the children back with her. This time she had taken Darryl and we needed to drive there and bring him back home. I hung up the phone and went to the cafeteria to eat. I ordered a steak because after receiving the news that I was about to receive my graduate degree I felt like a big shot and wanted to celebrate. I was so excited about all that had happened, however, that I only took a bite of my food before I got up and strolled away. I was thinking of a way to skip the graduation ceremony altogether and return home to my family. As a ploy, I asked for permission to go to Colorado to do some fishing and they said that it was okay. Of course I ended up going home to drive to Florida to pick up my son. I received my degree in the mail and though I didn't march, I was very pleased to have completed my goal.

The 1960s had definitely laid the foundation for so many promising things to look forward to. It was a time when blacks were beginning to be heard and when they were no longer willing to accept the backseat. We had lost some great leaders, but we had also made some huge progress. I had buried family members who were instrumental in molding me into the man I had become, though I still had a lot more growing to do. I had accomplished a lot of wonderful things and I was learning the tools necessary to be an effective leader. Chris and I had faced some difficult battles, but we always managed to overcome them. I have to salute the 1960s because the good times made me advance and the bad times made me stronger. It was time now to expand with an organization that I felt would be instrumental in educating black people about the political arena.

The Greenwood Voters' League had already sparked people's curiosity. I remember I was in the classroom teaching one day when I looked up and there was an unfamiliar man at the door. He was from the U.S. Justice Department and he was there to inquire about the Voters' League. I excused myself from the students and walked out to greet him. I gave him a brief summary of what the Voters' League represented. I encouraged him to come to the meeting on Wednesday nights and learn about it for himself. I had not been as heavily involved in the organization as I would have liked because of my commitment to earn a master's degree. But with that goal accomplished, I was ready now to devote the time and energy to the Greenwood Voters' League and I knew that it would pay dividends for Delta blacks in the end!

The Greenwood Voters' League

The Voting Rights Act that Congress passed in 1965 was a major civil rights breakthrough for the African American. The birth of the Greenwood Voters' League that immediately followed it became a power to be dealt with in Mississippi. When I accepted the responsibility of being president of this organization, it placed me in a position that I always wanted to be in. I wanted to lead black people in their quest to have an effective voice in their own community. I had watched in awe all the great milestones that occurred in the civil rights movement. I relished the fact that black people were taking a stand for equality and I knew my time would eventually come to have an effect on black progress in the Mississippi Delta. I had dedicated years to my own education to ensure that I had the credentials to navigate the direction that I wanted my life to go in. I was elected president in 1965 and it was now 1970, and the membership was growing. In the interim I had become more determined, more educated, and definitely more dedicated to the league's purpose.

My brother-in-law, Dr. Roosevelt Sisson, PhD in business, drew up the legal document setting up the constitution and the bylaws of the Greenwood Voters' League. These were requirements that had to be met in order to get the league charted. The purpose of the constitution was to make known to officers and members of the organization general information about certain accepted practices, rules, and regulations of the body. I understood that in order to operate effectively every organization needs guidelines, which gives direction to its operation. The members of the Greenwood Voters' League are firm believers in the power of the ballot and we vigorously encourage blacks to register to vote. We encourage members to elect both black and white representatives of their choice to public office. We urge them to exercise their full civic and national duties and responsibilities. When I first became president of the Voters' League, there were only forty black people voting in Leflore County. It was now well over a hundred people coming out every Wednesday to hear the political issues that affected their community. Many came to the meetings out of mere curiosity, just to hear about what was happening in the community. The annual membership fee was only two dollars and we paid five dollars each week to rent the building space. The treasury only had about three or four hundred dollars, but we didn't need much money since our expenses were always kept to a minimum. We had legal services backing us up if we had to go to court to solve any case of discrimination, and we didn't have to pay them high fees for their work. Individually I wasn't eligible for the free legal services, but I represented poor people who were entitled. We had young energetic lawyers on our team who were anxious to fight and break down racial barriers. So we had the legal muscle of highly regarded attorneys to tackle any issues that came onto our path. There were excellent lawyers during this time, people such as Willie Perkins, who is now my colleague in the legislature, Alex Sanders, Alvin Chambliss, and many more largely unknown but just as competent legal minds. These lawyers would not hesitate to sue anybody that warranted it.

I also had no problem with directly confronting white people on appropriate issues because of my own background. I was born and raised in the South on a plantation, but that didn't bother me. I had rubbed shoulders with many white students at the universities that I attended across the country. I had a strong will to get black people into places that they had never been before and this included numerous elective offices. Moreover, I wanted to see blacks appointed to boards and commissions, the real power bases in most local communities, and this became my primary focus as the leader of the Greenwood Voters' League.

The decade of the 1970s began quite favorably for the Jordan family. We had certainly experienced a lot of heartache and life-changing news throughout the 1960s and clearly it was time for a breather from life's problems. The children were growing up faster than we realized, but they were healthy and well-adjusted and for this we were blessed and most grateful. David Jr. and Joyce were in high school and Donald was in junior high. I had obtained a master's degree, but I was still looking to attend various institutes for courses sponsored by the National Science Foundation. Chris was also taking advantage of improving her knowledge of the science discipline. All teachers of science and mathematics across the country could receive scholarships to advance in these subject areas. Chris was already in the Greenwood school district, but I had not been fortunate enough to obtain employment in the only city I had called home. I was working in Holmes County in 1970, but I was looking to change that. It so happened that a misunderstanding turned into a blessing in disguise for me.

One day I came home from school and found Chris looking as if something was troubling her. I immediately asked her what had triggered the gloomy disposition. She stated that she didn't know if she still held her teaching position. Of course I didn't like the sound of that one bit, because I knew nothing could have warranted my wife being terminated. I looked at my watch and realized that we still had time to catch the superintendent in his office. We arrived at his office and I wasted no time getting to the point of my visit. I looked Dr. Dribben straight in the eye and asked him if Chris had been terminated. He told me that she had not been dismissed, but she had been transferred to an all-black school. School administrators had tried the team- teaching system to see if it would work—a black teacher and a white teacher together in an integrated classroom. Chris was teamed with a young white man. She held a degree in science and he did not. He felt intimidated by her qualifications and no longer wanted her teaching with him; as a result, she was transferred to another school. School officials wanted to pass it off claiming some other reason, but we were intelligent enough to read between the lines. I felt since we were in his office and my wife had already gotten the short end of the stick that I had nothing to lose in speaking my mind. I said, "Dr. Dribben, I have a master's degree in science and I'm trying to understand what it would take to get into the Greenwood public school system. I attended school here and I graduated from one of the district's high schools, and I don't understand."

Dr. Dribben finally heaved a deep sigh and said, "I tell you, Jordan, the problem is that no black principal will recommend you because they're intimidated by you." I was completely flabbergasted by his response. I quickly asked, "Afraid of me for what?" He said, "Let me give you a clearer understanding. I like you and I think you all have some nice children. I would love for the two of you to be at home teaching." Dr. Dribben made sure we had direct eye contact when he asked me to promise that if I was hired I would not give him any trouble. I looked him straight in the eye and said, "My primary concern is education and I have never deviated from that." I wanted to be sure that Dr. Dribben had a clear understanding of who he was hiring. I quickly informed him of my heavy involvement with the Voters' League and that I was the president of the organization. He claimed that he didn't have a problem with it and that he was only concerned with what transpired in the school classrooms. He picked up the telephone to make a call, but not before reiterating for me to stay clear of trouble. He placed a call to Mr. Solomon Outlaw, principal of L. H. Threadgill High School, while Chris and I remained in his office. Dr. Dribben said, "Mr. Outlaw, I have David Jordan in my office and I was wondering if you had an opening for a science teacher." I could hear him through the phone loud and clear saying, "Yes, sir." Dr. Dribben asked Mr. Outlaw if he would hire me. Mr. Outlaw said, "Yes, sir. He's a good man." It was that Mr. Outlaw had a position for me at this school. Chris and I left Dr. Dribben's office quite pleased because we were both finally teaching in Greenwood.

The summer of 1970 is when Chris left to take summer courses at Howard University. We also bought a brand-new Chevrolet Impala that same year. The kids and I drove up to Washington, D.C., and spent the last week with Chris at school. I enjoyed driving there with the kids because I loved showing them different places. I wanted their world to consist of more than just spending time in the Mississippi Delta, as had been my youth.

In the fall of 1970, I began my tenure in the Greenwood public school system. I was a teacher at L. H. Threadgill School, which was right down the street from my house. I was finally blessed with what I had sought for a number of my years in education and I certainly looked forward to the new experience. But all was not perfect as both black and white educators had to make adjustments to the desegregated reality. My own temperament was sorely tested at times. For example, there was a white principal at the junior high school named Mr. Bobby Fisher, working under Mr. Outlaw, with whom I had to clear up a major misunderstanding in order for us to have a decent working relationship. There was an elderly African American lady working at the school whom we called Ms. Annie. I can't remember her last name, but she was a sweet lady around seventy-five years old, who did custodial work. I recall how Mr. Fisher would get on the intercom and call her name. It was something about the way he said, "Annie, come to the office!" that I considered degrading and disrespectful. It was his way of getting her to come quickly to the office if he needed some chores completed. I didn't feel like it was acceptable to be calling her out like she was a slave in front of all the young black students. When we had our faculty meeting, I mentioned my concerns to the other faculty members. His wife and some of the other teachers actually resented me bringing the concern to the meeting. Mr. Fisher continued to call Ms. Annie in this disrespectful manner until I was forced to bring it directly to his attention. When I didn't get any results, I brought it to Mr. Outlaw's attention. He agreed that he would speak with Mr. Fisher, but nothing changed after our conversation. Mr. Fisher called her one time too many during a time when I was on break and I stormed into his office to confront him about it. I said, "I'm not going to allow you to continue to address this elderly woman like you have been doing. I've mentioned it in the faculty meeting and to your supervisor, but nothing has been resolved. If you keep doing it, then I'm going to have to take action against you, even if it means fighting for you to be moved to another school!" Mr. Fisher turned beet red, but I didn't give him a chance to respond and I walked out of his office. He finally stopped calling her in that manner; he found out what her last name was and began using it appropriately.

One of my most memorable periods at Threadgill occurred on the eve of Dr. King's birthday. As this date approached I wanted to have a celebration in remembrance of one of my greatest heroes. Mr. Fisher allowed me to play phonograph records containing speeches and an account of his life and work for all the students to hear for about an hour or so over the intercom. I was quite pleased that Mr. Fisher allowed me this opportunity to educate the students, black and white, about such a dynamic leader. Recognizing the human rights contributions of Dr. King on his birthday is not something that happened as easily at other Mississippi schools during this period.

I taught at Threadgill for one year and then the administration decided they needed a black teacher at the W. C. Williams School. I was once again teaching science to seventh- and eighth-graders. I had an advanced degree but equally important, they needed a black man to work closely with the black students because the school was integrated. I was a little disappointed about the transfer because I wanted to teach in the high school and I had been recommended twice to teach on that level. The senior high principal, Mr. John McHann, rejected me because he claimed that I would be a bad influence on the high school students. I didn't quite understand how the administration could draw this conclusion, especially since I was trained for high school teaching. It disappointed me because I believed I was being punished as a result of my involvement in the community. I learned early in life that preparation and timing were very important factors in advancing. I would know if, and when, the time came for me to fight for a position at the high school level. I knew, however, that if an opportunity presented itself I would be well prepared for it.

The principal at my school, Mr. Ward Jackson, made me his right-hand man. Each time there was a conflict, he would call me to the office to assist him in getting it resolved. There seemed to always be a little hostility between the black students and the white students. The students weren't accustomed to a black person teaching them, especially a black male. They spent the majority of their time just staring at me, but that didn't bother me. I looked at this as just another opportunity to grow in the profession because I always wanted to teach in an integrated school. My experience in Wyoming had definitely prepared me for a variety of challenges. I was naturally audacious, but I was also very confident in my ability and knowledge; I had placed myself in a great position professionally because of the amount of science I had on my resume, and school officials knew my preparedness and qualifications far exceeded that of most in the district. It took a few months for me to get comfortable in my new environment before I began making adjustments. The school administration updated the lab in order for me to demonstrate experiments and the students enjoyed and learned from them.

It wasn't long after school began that I was being left in administrative charge in Mr. Jackson's absence. I had no administrative experience nor did I receive any extra income for acting in a capacity as assistant principal. I had no desire to become a principal, but I enjoyed having certain larger responsibilities; I loved the idea of being able to step outside of my familiar surroundings anyway. It was indeed a good feeling that I was trusted enough to oversee things while he was away. Sometimes I got a little flack from a staff member or two, but it was nothing that I couldn't handle. I could get a little rough, if necessary, and I could also hold my own if a confrontation developed. Some teachers wanted to challenge my authority by finding excuses to be out of their classrooms. It didn't bother me that they were trying to take advantage of me because I was a classroom teacher like they were and I understood their thinking about testing the limits.

On Fridays things could get a little hectic because that was the day students could unleash their animosity and retaliate against each other for an offense they had previously experienced. Sometimes there was racial animus associated with the students' behavior. For example, after school the black students would try to catch up with the white students who had disrespected them during the week. I would be at one end of the street and Mr. Jackson would be at the other end waiting to diffuse any problems. Sometimes the duty would drain me, but it was well worth the exhaustion if it kept the violence under control.

At Threadgill school we took it literally, and seriously, when cleanup week rolled around and we all gathered together to clean up the community. A teacher and I would petition about 130 students and faculty members to march throughout the streets of Greenwood picking up garbage. We called it a "cleanup parade" and I had no problem taking the white teachers into the black community. I felt this showed a sign of unity and it was a good gesture of community service cleaning up the streets and lots in this collective manner.

In the summer of 1971 Chris received an opportunity to attend Ball State University in Muncie, Indiana. She was taking advantage of the opportunity to enroll in more advanced courses in her field of studies. I enjoyed that we again were able to travel and experience new things and new places and so did she, but we both knew that nothing was more fulfilling and gratifying to us than simply just being at home as a family.

There were certain issues that the Greenwood Voters' League wanted addressed to make blacks feel that we were continuing to move in a positive direction. I was strictly focused on what was in the best interest of the people, so I knew I was ready to push for qualified individuals to advance without race being a factor in disqualifying them in the hiring process. To this end the league wanted to see black people appointed to positions in the fire department, police department, and on the school board. The city council promised me that a black fireman would soon be hired and I was definitely looking forward to seeing that become a reality. I made requests for those running for office to speak at the Greenwood Voters' League. Those who felt they didn't have to comply would see we meant business when their names didn't appear on the endorsement sheet. Most office seekers soon came to realize that an endorsement from the Greenwood Voters' League carried a lot of weight.

In the meantime, in the summer break of 1972 I resumed enrolling in advanced courses. I had taken a two-year break from summer classes in order for Chris to take advantage of receiving advanced courses. I had also enjoyed bonding with the children over their summer break. I headed to the University of Texas in Austin and arrived to see a simply beautiful and impressive campus. I was quite relaxed because I had already taken courses above my earned master's degree. My work in Texas would be entirely for professional improvement purposes, which made things easier because it relieved me of a considerable amount of academic performance pressure. I had been offered a scholarship to work toward my PhD, but the dean wanted me to seek a business administration degree instead, primarily because the program needed to increase its enrollment, especially black graduate student enrollment. However, in order to work towards that degree, I would have to start with basic courses. The university business school was willing to pay twelve thousand dollars a year for me to relocate my family to Texas and pursue the business degree. It was a good stipend for just going to school, but I didn't find it particularly appealing; I didn't accept it because I had a science degree, a subject area that had been the focus of my interest for a long time and I did not look favorably on having to take so many basic business courses just to meet the standard of entering the graduate program. Moreover, we certainly were not looking to relocate, and this was of no minor concern in our decision.

When school was in full regular session, there were about forty thousand students in attendance, making the university the largest institution I had ever attended. There was also a little negative history attached to this school that was not easy for me to forget. In 1966 while I was in school in Kansas a real tragedy occurred on the Texas campus. A deranged student woke up one morning and killed his parents. He wasn't quite ready to end his violent tangent, so he went to the campus and took the lives of fifteen students. It was a horrific experience for the university and I can still remember well the headlines that the incident made. My roommate and I often visited the university balcony and stood on the same spot where the shooter committed his dastardly deed. His view from the balcony allowed him to see just about the whole campus, so it was easy for him to single out his victims. When my roommate and I didn't have any classes, we also often visited the state capitol, which was located near the university campus. We would listen to the debates going on in the senate, inspired to do so because Barbara Jordan, no kin, was a senator during this time. I remember she was Texas governor for a day and on this day I got an opportunity to meet her. She was a great lady who cared deeply about her duties and her constituents and it was an honor to meet her.

My time at the University of Texas went by quickly and it was soon time to get back into the classroom. I returned home to discover that a black fireman had not been hired as promised by the city council, and this greatly disappointed me. I quickly reached out to my group and headed to the commissioner's office. The people who accompanied me were Mr. S. N. Dickerson, a retired mail carrier, Rev. B. T. McSwine, and the vice president of the Voters' League, Louis Golden. I had always been the spokesperson, most of the membership feeling it appropriate anyway since I was the president and an effective communicator. I had some fire in me and addressing issues of discrimination didn't intimidate me one bit. When we got inside the boardroom to see the commissioner and the mayor, I wasted no time getting to the point. I wanted to know what happened to the promise of hiring a black fireman. The commissioner, Mr. C. E. Wright, said, "David, we'll have a black fireman by October 1." It was good hearing that, but the fire chief quickly intervened and said, "I'm not going to make white people in Greenwood mad by hiring a Negro fireman!" Our form of government consisted of a mayor and two commissioners and they reassured us that a black fireman would in fact be hired. I had no choice but to take their word and see what transpired.

It was October 1, 1972, when Greenwood got its first black fireman, a man by the name of James Elliot. We were elated over the hiring and we had him come to the Voters' League where he was welcomed by a packed house. It was now time to deal with the county to get a black deputy hired. There was a forum held at the high school for all of the white candidates running for sheriff of Leflore County. They wouldn't appear before the Voters' League, which forced me to meet them in their own territory. My purpose in doing so was to find out their views about blacks being hired to certain positions. I would bluntly ask each of them if they were elected sheriff would they hire a black deputy. All of the candidates said no, with the exception of Rufus Freeman. I was impressed with his response and asked him if he would come to speak before the Voters' League. Personally, he had no problem with my request, but his team advised against it. His team visited my home and we debated for over an hour about the importance of him showing up at the Voters' League meeting. I was finally able to convince him that it was the only way he could gain our support. His team tried to dictate to me what questions were appropriate to ask Mr. Freeman, but I wasn't going to allow that kind of interference. I did, however, promise to keep the meeting under control.

A crowd of over two hundred people gathered to await the candidate's arrival. He was familiar with a lot of the black people present and they definitely knew him. Most liked Freeman because he treated blacks with dignity and respect. He confirmed at the meeting that he would have no problem hiring a black if he was elected. He swept the county vote by a high margin and, true to his word, hired the first black deputy, Charlie Cooley. We were so proud of Charlie walking into one of our meetings with the big star on his clothing. He was a board member and he often came to the Voters' League meeting still dressed in his uniform. He would have his big gun on his side and a western hat sitting on top of his head. Perhaps

Charlie looked even more distinguished than he actually was because we had never seen a black man in his position before in our county. His accomplishment made the whole community extremely proud of him.

Black Greenwood had an African American man in the fire department, a recently hired meter reader, and now a black deputy sheriff. The next order of business was to work on getting a black assigned to the all-white school board. We had something really incredible going on with our successes and the Voters' League was attracting the attention of people from all over the state. It soon became common knowledge that people running for public office would benefit from an endorsement by the Greenwood Voters' League. It was no secret that I wanted blacks appointed to boards and commissions, regardless of what it took to achieve the goal. Previously, whites were never required to come to the black community and answer to us for anything. I was a maladjusted teacher and community activist who was requiring this as a prerequisite to get an endorsement from the Voters' League; things had certainly changed now for the betterment of all of our citizenry and this pleased me immensely.

The city of Greenwood suffered a flood at the end of 1972, right before the Christmas holiday, and all of the state officials came to the city to speak to the citizens in a special gathering about helping us. One of the U.S. senators was present and the lieutenant governor was also in attendance. When the meeting ended, I made my way to the lieutenant governor and asked him if he would be interested in attending a Voters' League meeting. He agreed and I made preparation for him to appear on the scheduled date. I knew it was an honor to have a lieutenant governor speak to any group in Greenwood and the idea that it was the Voters' League made it that much more significant. The meeting was held at a school with a full capacity of over two hundred people. Lieutenant Governor William Winter spoke to the crowd about his responsibilities as an officeholder and talked eloquently about the importance of education in moving Mississippi forward. He was a big advocate of education because he was a highly educated man himself. He discussed ways in which the school

Cleveland Jordan, father

Elizabeth Tate Jordan, mother

Clevester Jordan, brother

Will Henry Jordan, brother

Andrew L. Jordan, brother

Viola Jordan, sister

David L. Jordan, 1970s

Malouf Store (on the left) and Night Club (lower right) in the Rising Sun community in Greenwood, Mississippi, of the 1940s

Cotton gin where Jordan worked from 1942 until 1952; Whittington Plantation, four miles south of Greenwood, Mississippi

Day laborers picking cotton on Marcella Plantation, Mileston, Mississippi Delta, ca. 1939. Photograph by Marion Post Wolcott. Library of Congress, Prints & Photographs Division, FSA/OWI Collection.

Mule Race, 1942, Legion Field on Carrollton Avenue in Greenwood, Mississippi

Jordans' house on the Whittington Plantation

David Jordan in the US Army, May 17, 1959

Christine Bell Jordan and David L. Jordan, June 1975

David Jordan Jr. and Joyce Jordan, the oldest of four children of David and Christine Jordan, who is pregnant with their third child , Donald Jordan. David Sr. was in the US Army during 1959.

David L. Jordan Jr., oldest son   Joyce Jordan Dugar, daughter

Family celebrating David and Christine's birthday, April 3, 2009, at Yianni's Restaurant in Greenwood, Mississippi. Seated from left to right: Sela, Chris, David, and Viola. Standing from left to right: Heir, Hope Lindsay, Loren, Donald, Jennifer, and Darryl.

First grandchildren, Larry Dugar Jr. and Stephanie Dugar

Emmett Till Memorial Marker, Money, Mississippi, ten miles north of Greenwood, Mississippi

Dr. Donald Jordan and Dr. Darryl Jordan with their father, (center)

Jordan's home during the 1960s. In 1962 SNCC workers Sam Block, Lawrence Guyot, and Luvaughn Brown took refuge in Jordan's home after being chased by armed white men.

Congressional Record

United States of America

PROCEEDINGS AND DEBATES OF THE 102ᵈ CONGRESS, FIRST SESSION

Vol. 137   WASHINGTON, TUESDAY, SEPTEMBER 24, 1991   No. 133

House of Representatives

CELEBRATION OF THE 25TH AN-NIVERSARY OF THE VOTERS LEAGUE OF GREENWOOD, MS

HON. MIKE ESPY
OF MISSISSIPPI
IN THE HOUSE OF REPRESENTATIVES
Tuesday, September 24, 1991

MVSU students waiting outside of Leflore County Circuit Clerk's office to get registered to vote, March 1975

Tribute in the *Congressional Record*, an honor presented to the Greenwood Voters' League by Congressman Mike Espy, September 24, 1991

The late Governor Cliff Finch poses with Voters' League members after making a speech in 1978

President Jimmy Carter, October 1977, at the White House, Washington, D.C.

President Bill Clinton, May 10, 2000, White House, Washington, D.C.

President Barack Obama, March 10, 2008, Jackson State University, Jackson, Mississippi. During roll call at the Democratic National Convention, Denver, Colorado, I cast Mississippi votes for President Obama, August 27, 2008.

Watching senate election returns in 1992

Ward 6 Councilman David Jordan in 1985

Allegiance to the flag debate in 2001

Governor Haley Barbour signs the Mississippi Blues Bill, authored by Senator Jordan. From the *Greenwood Commonwealth*, April 27, 2004.

Greenwood City Hall

Civil rights march, downtown Greenwood, Mississippi, 2005

In response to comments made by Jordan after the rescreening of a 1966 NBC documentary about race in Greenwood, someone shot into the Jordans' home and Chris's car, 2011.

system could improve to meet the educational needs of Mississippi students. It was a grand occasion, one that I will never forget.

It had come to the point where many people were watching my evolving influence as president and spokesman for the Voters' League. Milestones were being set in Leflore County through the work of the league and this was good for all the citizens, black and white. As my influence increased, naturally my name began to circulate throughout the state as a significant force in the Mississippi political arena. I knew the day would eventually come when I would be even more prominent in the public eye. But there were clearly consequences for me personally. As the league's most visible leader I was adored by some, hated by others. Unfortunately there were some white people who were starting to feel that I was trying to take things away from them. I couldn't understand why they felt this way when they had always had more than their share of everything. It goes without really having to say that their logic was certainly misguided. I was content and confident in my ability to endure all the obstacles that came with being on the front line, however. I was energetic and determined to achieve as much black progress as I could through the Voters' League. My motivation was heightened by my desires for my own family; I wanted my children to live in a world where race would not be a determining factor in how far they climbed up the ladder of success. My kids were getting older now and Chris and I wanted them to be able to capitalize on every opportunity available to them!

Wings to Fly

There were many wonderful experiences that had occurred thus far in my life, but nothing gave me greater satisfaction than the joy that my children brought me. From the moments of their births, Chris and I had always been strongly committed to the welfare of our children. We wanted to insure that they had every resource available to reach their highest potential. We didn't care what professions our children chose, as long as they knew there was no goal unattainable. The love of my family had always made the rough spots turn smooth and dim situations have light. I wanted my children not to be afraid of competitive situations because of their skin color. Chris and I were extremely proud that two of our children were among the first to integrate the Greenwood public school system. It gave them confidence early that they could be the first to break through barriers and feel comfortable knowing that they belonged. My wife and children were my inspiration for every step that I had taken in my fight for justice. I wanted them to be proud of their father and more than ever I wanted to make sure they had wings and could fly. Chris and I had provided a stable family environment for our children to achieve anything that their hearts desired.

We were approaching a wonderful time in our lives and that was the graduation of our two oldest children. David Jr. and Joyce were only steps away from receiving their high school diplomas and on to the next stepping stone in their lives. Joyce had received a scholarship to Mississippi Valley State College. She was following in her parents' footsteps by attending the same college and majoring in science. Joyce was a member of the marching band and had decided to live on campus. I was extremely proud of my baby girl and it made us feel good to know that we had set a solid path for her to follow. Joyce still had the enthusiastic attitude that she had as a little girl and she was eager to start college. David, on the other hand, wasn't too keen on the idea of attending Valley State College. He actually received a football scholarship; the coaches had vigorously recruited him because they really wanted him to be a member of the football team, but he wanted to attend the University of Wyoming. I knew the climate out there was too cold in the winter and I knew it was just too far away from home. David decided to give Valley State a shot and attended the school, though for only one semester because he just didn't like it. He eventually got a job working as a bricklayer building homes. I told him that we couldn't allow him to live under our roof and not attend college. Chris and I were big advocates of higher education because we knew it was instrumental in opening up doors for life advancement.

One day he walked in the door and casually said, "Daddy, I want you to sign me up for the navy." I said, "Okay." David entered the navy and served a term of four years. He occasionally came home on furlough, but he was determined to have a life away from the Mississippi Delta. I admired his courage in not being afraid to tackle the unknown. He had watched me explore different cities and different opportunities and he wanted a chance to do the same. I felt confident that both of my children would be fine as they approached adulthood. I wanted them to experience life, but also to remember that we were always just a phone call away.

African Americans were continuously moving forward, making more progress than we had ever made in Greenwood. We soon added another black fireman and another black deputy to these important public services. I felt good because the Voters' League had been responsible for helping make this progress a reality; we had been determined not to deviate from our mission of having blacks hired in jobs that had traditionally locked us out. I felt it was time for a black person to serve on the city school board and making this happen became the focus of the league's next endeavor. The president of the school board had Mr. Louis Golden, the vice president of the Voters' League, get in touch with me. He wanted to meet with the appropriate league committee designated to address this issue. So, Mr. Golden and another league member and I traveled to his office. The men on our committee were older gentlemen in their fifties and sixties. I was the youngest in the group, but they considered me to be the spokesperson for the Greenwood Voters' League. These men embraced me and protected my vulnerability when necessary. They knew I was articulate and confident enough to handle the interest of our people.

When we stepped into the office of the president of the school board, he immediately got to the business at hand. He said, "David Jordan, I will resign from the school board to open up a spot for a black person. I feel a black should get a chance to represent black citizens on the school board." I thought this was very unusual because here was a white man who was willing to resign from his position to allow black representation, something that was proper and right politically and morally, but his ethical gesture was not prompted by demand from the league committee. Like a whirlwind, news of the president's overture reached the Voters' League and the press soon picked up on it as well. The school board president, who was the owner of a local farm equipment store, had gained my admiration and respect and that of other forward-thinking blacks in Greenwood. He later met with Dr. Dribben and shared with him his intention to resign his position on the board in order for a black person to have an opportunity to serve. There was no final decision that came from the meeting, so the Voters' League members eventually met with Dr. Dribben. We sat around his office and I could feel his eyes staring intensely at me. In the most strident voice, Dr. Dribben exclaimed, "David Jordan, I want you to remember that I run the school system!" I chuckled under my breath because I had certainly not forgotten his position. I simply stated, "We're just trying to work this situation out and get some representation on the school board." He then reminded me of the promise that I wouldn't attack him if I was hired in the public school system. I wanted him to truly understand that this was by no means a personal attack against him. The fact that we were asking for a black person to be on the board had nothing to do with the president volunteering to give up his seat. I informed him that we were there to discuss this matter with him and that our next stop would be city hall. It took no time for the news to be released that David Jordan was pushing for a black to be appointed to the school board.

The mayor and the commissioners had no problem with my request, but they wanted the right person for the position. The next day, Mr. L. H. Threadgill came to my classroom. He said, "Mr. Jordan, I was informed by Dr. Dribben that you are seeking a black person to serve on the school board." Mr. Threadgill was now a retired principal; he had been my principal during the entire time I had attended public school in Greenwood and I served under him during my student teaching job in the system, so we knew each other well. I informed him that the information he had was indeed correct. Dr. Dribben wanted us to appoint Mr. Threadgill to the position and I agreed to take it back to the committee to get their feedback. They decided that they preferred someone else. I suggested a black man who was a good friend of mine, but he wasn't a registered voter. You couldn't serve on the board unless you were registered to vote and I was completely stunned to find out that he wasn't. We finally decided that we wanted Mr. W. J. Bishop for the position. At the time he was working for Malouf Music Company. The mayor didn't want him to serve because he had participated in a boycott after the assassination of Dr. King. Following Dr. King's death there had been a six-month boycott in Greenwood protesting the lack of blacks on committees and boards. The committee couldn't believe that city officials were trying to hold this against Mr. Bishop and we brought the information back to the Voters' League. They also couldn't believe that they were using such a ridiculous excuse against Mr. Bishop. I went back to the mayor's office and insisted that Mr. Bishop was the person we wanted for the job. We battled back and forth until we finally reached an agreement.

At the next meeting by city officials Mr. Bishop was appointed to the board. We felt that this was a huge step and the fact that we didn't deviate from who we wanted was really a big accomplishment. The next issue that the league had to confront was with the county over its move to build a living plantation to depict the period from 1850 to 1875. The architect who planned to build the plantation wanted to come before the Voters' League to explain to us how it was going to be built and what it would mean to the economy. He told us that black people would be performing as slaves on a live plantation. I immediately interjected and said on behalf of myself and the Voters' League that we were opposed to the idea. I couldn't believe that they were attempting to rub our faces in the mud again with slavery. I said, "We have already given 247 years to slavery, and now in 1973 to come back and attempt to get us to play slaves on a living plantation is ridiculous!" All the members joined in and supported me in my strong stand against this plan for the county to make money by degrading its black citizens.

The Voters' League went on official record as opposing this idea. We talked to state representative Robert Huggins and he told the governor about our disapproval of the project. The governor agreed with us and stated that he wouldn't allow it to happen. He said they could build a plantation, but there would not be any slave quarters. The decision resulted in the head of the county board of supervisors and me getting into a heated battle over the issue. The media made sure our disagreement was public. I said that if supporters wanted to see slaves then they could act out the part themselves. I reminded them that the South lost the Civil War and there was no reason to try to reproduce it other than to embarrass the black race. Governor Bill Waller had compassion for our concern and agreed with me that the plantation issue would reopen old racial wounds that had not totally healed. He said he would not sign the bill dealing with the state's involvement with the proposal until organizers deleted the provision concerning the slave quarters. We won the fight though a lot of controversy followed the victory. Other than the satisfaction of defeating a measure that was not in the best interest of Mississippi, my only other personal gratification from this entire fight was that the governor and I built an everlasting bond over it. I came to relish and respect this relationship perhaps more than I did with any other powerful white political leader in the state.

In the summer of 1975, I accepted an opportunity to teach at Mississippi Valley State University. It was a great experience to be teaching at this higher level, especially since I wasn't allowed to teach at the high school level. The chemistry teacher at the university went away to obtain some advanced schooling to enhance his teaching and he recommended that I fill his position while he was gone since I held a master's degree. Although he returned from sabbatical the next year, the department head wanted to add to the chemistry faculty and he recommended me for the permanent teaching position. I was honored by the offer, but I would never quit my job in the city system to go to the university because I was making more money in the Greenwood system. Although it had only been temporary, it was a great accomplishment for me personally and professionally to have taught at the same college where I received my undergraduate degree. It was a brief reminder of how far I had come, but I knew there was still a lot more for me to accomplish.

In the same summer of 1975 Governor Waller's time in office was nearing an end. This was a period in state history when a governor could not succeed himself in office. Waller was now running for the U.S. Senate, and this allowed me to invite him to the Voters' League. It was Father's Day Sunday when he came to speak. I will never forget the helicopter landing on the high school football field and the governor and his fifteen-year-old son stepping out. (His son now serves as chief justice of the Mississippi Supreme Court, and I visit him occasionally to talk about the good old days. I always remind him about how much admiration I had for his father because he attempted to put Medgar Evers's killer behind bars.) There were over seven hundred people waiting to greet the governor in the gymnasium at Threadgill School. It was such a glorious and prestigious program; people in Greenwood couldn't believe that I was responsible for the governor being in the city.

There was one person in particular who was completely shocked that white candidates were coming to speak at the Voters' League.

This was Dr. George Lane, a black physician who had moved from Greenwood to Milwaukee during the civil rights struggles. He was in the city when Governor Waller came before the league, and I made sure that he shook hands with the governor. Governor Waller's appearance validated the important role the Greenwood Voters' League was starting to play in the state's political life, for it was becoming common knowledge that everyone across the state seeking political office was coming to the Voters' League for endorsement, and it didn't matter what party they represented or what their racial orientation was.

In 1976 we were forced to boycott a department store named Gibson's. The company was based out of Louisiana and consisted of a chain of stores that carried a variety of goods similar to Walmart's. Although there were black employees, none worked in a position that allowed them to interact with customers or handle money. For example, the company simply refused to hire African Americans as cashiers. One Saturday the manager of the Greenwood store fired a black employee because of a minor disagreement between them. I got involved when the worker talked to me concerning the matter; I just didn't feel the issue was serious enough to warrant his termination, so I decided to go to the store and speak with the manager about it and about a couple of other issues that needed addressing. He was in the company of two other white employees when I approached him. I asked if I could speak with him for a few minutes and he agreed. Getting to the point immediately, I politely asked him to hire some black cashiers and to consider rehiring the person who was fired. He looked at me and bluntly said that he would do neither. He said that he actually resented my attempting to question his position and his authority. I realized that, with his attitude, talking to him was a waste of time and I needed to take it a step further. We started a picket line the Saturday morning before Easter Sunday. Our signs clearly indicated that it was the Greenwood Voters' League leading the boycott and as we informed potential black shoppers about our cause, we persuaded many of them not to enter the store. Most of them thought well enough about what we were doing to honor the boycott and they immediately turned around and headed back to their cars. Besides me, it was Chris, Donald, and a few others who manned the picket line. We stayed until the 9:00 p.m. closing time. Although the atmosphere outside of the store was not normal, it was never so charged that we felt threatened or intimidated. The police would circle around the premises continuously in order to keep the peace and this gave us some assurance about our safety.

There were always at least two people continuously on the picket line and though we knew the commitment required sacrifice, the league gave additional incentive by paying the men about forty dollars a week for their participation. I taught during the day, but after I went home and relaxed for a while I went back to the store and stayed on the picket line until closing. There were other Greenwood-area blacks whose curiosity brought them to the site, but they didn't join us in the picketing. They were just interested in seeing how this situation was going to turn out. It bothered me a little that there were a few black people who were critical of what we were doing, but I understood it was impossible to get unanimity regardless of how just the cause. A number of local whites who employed black workers would have them come to the Voters' League meeting in an effort to persuade me to end the boycott, but I refused to give in unless and until I was promised some positive results.

A few white officers got into a verbal exchange with some of the civil rights activists working in our community. One night a group of police officers came rushing from the Greenwood police station to the boycott vicinity. They went to the back of the store and climbed up on the roof. They claimed there had been a sniper spotted on top of the building, but we knew this was just a means of trying to get us away from the store front and we weren't budging.

The boycott lasted for six months and during that time there were many confrontations. A black lady who had originally asked us to boycott the store turned against us and cursed us out. Some blacks who wanted us to stop picketing shouted harsh words at us indicating in the clearest way their disapproval of our efforts. We even encountered a group that broke through the picket line and, understandably, that caused a little commotion. One old man, popularly referred to by his nickname of "Two Sticks," was as mean as a rattlesnake. He was committed to the cause and would curse people if they attempted to break the line. He called them "ignorant niggers" in the most strident tone. Though I understood his frustration and anger, I had to caution him not to react in such a manner. I often calmed him down by simply patting him on his shoulder; sometimes he listened, but unfortunately there were other times that his emotions really got the best of him and he couldn't be easily quieted. On one occasion a lady he cursed out called the authorities on him to have him arrested and she later pressed charges against him. In the court session I had to testify on his behalf. I explained to the court about the righteousness of our cause and the peaceful nature of the boycott. I emphasized that the participants had not broken any laws. My testimony was apparently convincing, but there actually was no evidence to convict Two Sticks. The judge placed the complaint in the file where it remains to this day.

The boycott continued, and I remember staring at the words that were written on the pavement in white chalk. I knew we were doing the right thing when I saw that someone had written in big letters, "Business is better since niggers stop coming!" It became clearer than ever that we had to take a stand and gain the respect that we deserved as human beings or else we would continue to be disrespected and overlooked when it came to local job opportunities.

During the fifth month of the boycott Byron De La Beckwith visited the store. The workers didn't know who he was, so I told them that he was the man who was responsible for the death of Medgar Evers. I guess he was considered a hero to some of the whites in town because whenever there was something they considered a racial problem they would send for him. At this particular time, I had a legal permit to carry a weapon. I went to the trunk of my car and retrieved my .38 caliber gun because I knew how dangerous this man was. I'm thinking, if this man walks in my direction I would have to shoot him. The other guys on the picket line followed my lead and went to get their weapons as well. De La Beckwith walked inside of the store and began communicating with the guard. He kept his eye on us and pointed in our direction as he engaged in his conversation. He eventually came outside and walked close to our space. His beady eyes watched us like a hawk and his disposition became extremely cocky. I kept my finger on the trigger of my gun that was in my pocket because I was not sure of what he would actually do. He probably sensed that I had something in my pocket to deal with him because of the way he was observing me. He jumped into his truck and told us that we had better not still be outside when sundown came. He gave us one final look and then sped off. We had come too far to allow his threats to intimidate us, so we ignored him and continued our mission. As a way to further thwart our efforts some white teachers would demand that students get a special notebook that could only be purchased at the local Gibson store. The ploy, however, did not work. I admired the fact that the students and their parents supported the cause strongly enough that they were willing to drive twenty-eight miles to the next town to get the required supplies. There was also a white man who drove up with his wife and questioned me concerning the boycott. When I explained to him what we were doing and why, he began cursing me. He jumped out of his car and came charging in my direction, but the two men in my company restrained him and sent him on his way.

By September the district manager had come from Louisiana to meet with me and the other members of the boycott. We explained to him that we simply wanted black cashiers to be hired. He promised if we pulled the boycott that he would oblige our request by hiring black cashiers and he stuck to his word. The boycott soon ended and once again justice prevailed. The boycott almost broke the Greenwood Voters' League financially, but we eventually had a fundraiser to replenish the treasury. We celebrated another victory and for the Greenwood Voters' League, it was definitely a major milestone. I was completely thrilled with the direction in which we were headed, and I felt confident that we would conquer many more hurdles. We were taking things step by step and accomplishing more than we could have ever imagined. I was elated about being the head of an organization that was becoming more powerful with each passing day. Black people were definitely making progress, and although we had a lot more issues to tackle, I felt confident knowing that we were on the right track to meaningful change. I knew that if we continued to stick together, nothing could slow us down. I also knew that I was being watched by many, for both good and bad purposes, and that my position as the president of the league had definitely increased my political clout.

The Political Scene

The year 1976 was significant for the Mississippi Democratic political party because it was the year that African Americans became a part of the state organization. It also marked the first time the Democrats effectively achieved racial integration. The newly elected governor, Cliff Finch, was responsible for bringing the Democratic Party together. The Democrats had been split along racial lines for many years, but those days were now a thing of the past. I ran for a seat in the Democratic caucus in Leflore County and I won on the county level. We went to the district after this election, party activists from the second congressional district meeting in the small nearby town of Winona. The state-level Democratic meeting would follow the district activity. When we got an opportunity to meet in the district, my colleagues included the legendary Mrs. Fannie Lou Hamer, who was willing to support my candidacy for the state committee, Aaron Henry, another civil rights icon who was the head of the Mississippi NAACP, and Hardy Lott, the Greenwood school board attorney. Many of the candidates who were running for office would come to the Voters' League seeking political backing. This was also the year that Jimmy Carter ran for the presidency of the United States. I was selected for the statewide Democratic Executive Committee to elect Carter and I attended the district meetings. I also conducted meetings at the Voters' League in support of Carter. So, at virtually every level established in behalf of the Carter candidacy, I was actively involved.

In October of 1976, Jimmy's wife, Rosalynn Carter, along with Mississippi's two U.S. senators, came to Greenwood for a rally. Whitt Monger, a local attorney and member of the party's executive committee, and I were asked to gather ten people to greet Mrs. Carter when her plane landed at the airport. There were a number of elderly women in the Voters' League. One woman in particular, whom we called "Mama Chestnut," could be quite vocal about certain issues. She was short in stature, but her height didn't keep her from making sure her voice was heard loud and clear. Mama Chestnut referred to me as her son and I wanted her to be one of the people who received an opportunity to meet Mrs. Carter. I asked her to go through her closet and pick out her best outfit and I reminded her to be certain to leave her tobacco at home. Another choice was an English teacher at Mississippi Valley State University. She was a professional woman and I didn't have to give any pointers to her about behavior or appropriate attire. A few other board members made up my total of five people; Mr. Monger's five were professional white people. We arrived at the airport around 4:00 p.m. and waited patiently for Mrs. Carter's plane to land. It wasn't long before a very outgoing woman stepped off the plane. I reminded Mama Chestnut to remain calm, but when she laid eyes on Mrs. Carter she immediately forgot what I had said. She began hollering, "There she is!" She finally grabbed Mrs. Carter and wrapped her arms tightly around her shoulders. Mrs. Carter smiled and politely returned the warm embrace. It became a defining moment for Mama Chestnut. I guess if anyone deserved to embrace the future First Lady it was Mama Chestnut because she was herself a great woman. We headed to the Youth Center in Greenwood and participated in a big rally. There was a band performing the Democrats' victory song, which was "Happy Days Are Here Again!" We had a great time and celebrated for over an hour until it was time for Mrs. Carter and her companions to leave for their next destination.

There was also a candidate by the name of Fred Harris of Oklahoma who was running for the Democratic Party's presidential nomination. He came to the Voters' League and appeared before a huge crowd. The candidates who came to speak to the Voters' League were putting our organization in the forefront of similar political and civic groups. I had the governor, lieutenant governor, state senators, and other political figures speak to the Voters' League. I was proud to be moving among all these people at a crucial period of our country's history. When I had no state people coming before the league, then I would call on local people. The Voters' League had a lot of activities going on, but at the same time I was still committed to my position as a teacher.

In November 1976 Jimmy Carter was elected president of the United States. He had served two years as a Georgia state senator and one term as governor of Georgia. He defeated Gerald Ford to become the thirty-ninth president of the United States. President Ford had been the vice president under Richard Nixon and had completed Nixon's remaining two and a half years once the president resigned in disgrace in August of 1974. Nixon was the first president in American history to resign from office, prompted by his involvement in the infamous Watergate scandal, which began with a break-in at the Democratic National Committee headquarters in Washington, D.C. There were tape recordings revealing that President Nixon had attempted to cover up the break-in. He was close to facing impeachment, so he resigned from office. After his resignation, Gerald Ford issued Nixon a pardon, insuring that he didn't serve any jail time.

In January of 1977, I received a personal invitation from the Carter administration to attend the inauguration. I was concerned about being able to get excused from work, but things worked in my favor. It was an honor for me to be attending this event and I was even able to contact Washington for a couple of extra passes. I wanted one more board member, Willie Dillard, to be able to attend. He was elated to be going because he had wanted an opportunity to meet the new president. We began our journey to Washington by taking a four-hour bus ride from Greenwood to Jackson, Mississippi, because of the snow. Chris stayed behind with the children, but I knew that she would be watching the event on television. I met all my other colleagues from the Democratic Party at the airport and we boarded a plane headed to the national capital. We arrived and got settled in our hotel in the midst of an electric atmosphere. It was hard to believe that I was actually in Washington at the request of the president. This was another personal milestone in my life and I was proud of it. I met with other politicians there from Mississippi and we enjoyed the politically eventful times together. The next day we attended a prayer breakfast led by "Daddy" King. This was my first time ever meeting Dr. Martin Luther King's father and it was indeed a pleasure. The day of the inauguration was cold and sunny, and it was truly amazing to witness President Carter and the First Lady walking down Pennsylvania Avenue.

In the spring of 1977 Chris and I watched another one of our children leave the nest. Donald graduated from high school and was attending Xavier University in New Orleans. He received a scholarship, majoring in premed, and we were extremely proud of him as we were with all of our children. At Xavier, Donald had the opportunity to meet author Alex Haley. Haley, who became famous for his novel *Roots*, was the guest speaker at Donald's graduation ceremony. We were a close-knit family and watching the children grow up and leave was not an easy thing to readily accept. It was rewarding that they were following in their parents' footsteps by majoring in science. There was one child left in the house now and that was Darryl. It would only be a matter of time before he too would soon be leaving to further his education.

Later in the summer, President Carter visited the state of Mississippi. I was invited to meet with him in Jackson at the Ramada Inn. I was able to shake hands with him and we took photos that made most of the state's newspapers. When it was time for school to start, a few teachers posted the clippings of me and the president in their classrooms. They wanted the students in the school to know that I had met the president of the United States. I didn't place any pictures on my door or in my classroom because I didn't want to appear boastful, but having met with the president and having the meeting pictorially acknowledged in these various ways was the thrill of my life, with the exception of the election and reelection of Barack Obama as president of the United States.

In this same year, I, along with other board members from the

Voters' League, sued the city of Greenwood. I had the support of Ms. Sammie Chestnut and Mr. Robert Sims to change the form of city government in order for blacks to be represented. We had to prove the existence of a pattern of discrimination and we definitely could show that. We felt confident that the ruling would be in our favor, whenever the decision was reached.

In September of 1978, I was subpoenaed to testify in federal court in Washington, D.C., in a Mississippi redistricting plan. I had been to court so many times in Mississippi that our attorney, Frank Parker, requested my presence in Washington. Mr. Bennie Thompson, who was an alderman in Bolton, Mississippi, at the time, was also summoned to testify. I assumed that I was going to be there for one day, but I ended up staying five days. I had packed only one suit, so I had to go shopping for clothes. I concluded my obligation in Washington and returned to Greenwood.

A month later I received an invitation from President Carter inviting me to the White House. He wanted me to be part of a meeting with a number of other southern leaders. I was included in the group of African American and Caucasian elected officials. I didn't know if the school district would allow me to attend this meeting, especially since I had only recently returned from Washington. I decided to approach Mr. Bishop concerning the matter. He was a member of the school board and I believed that he would have a little insight and an appreciation for the importance of the president's invitation. I explained to him the subject of the invitation and its importance, then handed him the letter validating everything that I had just told him. Mr. Bishop made a copy of the letter and assured me not to worry because I would definitely be attending. He went to speak with the district's superintendent and I returned to my classroom. A half hour later Mr. Bishop was at my classroom door beckoning for me to step into the hallway. He was happy to inform me that he had received permission for me to go to Washington, D.C. Lastly, I had to be cleared by the FBI, which did not appear to be a problem since I had never been in any trouble before. I remember the principal's voice coming through the intercom saying, "Mr. Jordan, report to the office! The White House is on the line!" You could see the surprised expression on the faces of the students and teachers to learn that the White House was calling for me. I drove to Memphis and met with some of my colleagues who were in the state Democratic Party. The head of the NAACP and a city councilman from Greenville were also present. We finally boarded the plane and after we arrived in Washington, D.C., that night I went straight to my hotel and called Chris to let her know that I had arrived safely. She knew that I was quite excited about having been personally invited by the president to attend this meeting and my enthusiasm about the expected outcome was also obvious to her.

The next morning I, along with black leaders from all over the South, met with President Carter. The president wanted his staff to discuss with us strategies that would improve the life of African Americans living in the South. We met with his whole cabinet and enjoyed speakers such as United Nations ambassador Andrew Young and Illinois state comptroller Roland Burris. It was a very enlightening experience and I was happy to be included in such an elite group of people. I remember a reporter asking me how I had been chosen to receive an invitation to the White House meeting. I had no problem informing him that I had been invited by the president of the United States. My chest was stuck out proudly and the people who knew me were also proud of my inclusion and recognition.

I felt the ripple effects of my inclusion in this White House gathering almost as soon as I got back to Mississippi. I began to receive invitations from all over the city to attend luncheons and various other functions. Leaders of some community organizations wanted to show their appreciation and gratitude for my representing Greenwood in Washington, D.C. Many of them had never heard of a black man being invited to the White House before and I was definitely the first one from Greenwood. All of this generated a great deal of publicity for a black man during this time and it certainly raised a lot of eyebrows outside of Leflore County as well. The recognition was definitely an honor for the school where I taught. The Voters' League continued to back me 100 percent; it was quite evident that I was making my way on the national scene and the league was basking in the limelight along with me!

The national Democratic Party held a midwinter meeting in Memphis and for the first time I met future president Bill Clinton. At age thirty-two, he had just been elected governor of Arkansas, the youngest governor in the country. As governor, Clinton was responsible for improving the educational system in Arkansas and became a leading figure among the so-called "New Democrats" who concentrated on welfare reform and smaller government. Governor Clinton was one of the speakers at the conference, along with Massachusetts senator Edward "Ted" Kennedy. It was indeed a pleasure to be at a meeting with a member of the famous Kennedy family.

While in Memphis I attended another meeting with a group of Hispanics. They asked me if I would vote with them in their effort to secure a spot on the Civil Rights Committee. The whole room was filled with Hispanics and they informed me that if I voted for them they would vote to have me elected to the committee. I thought it was a good gesture, so I agreed and gave them my full name. I didn't think much about it until I was elected to the Civil Rights Committee of the national Democratic Party. I was as light as a feather when I returned to Greenwood because I had had such a fulfilling experience. The local press had already picked up the story of my success and featured it along with my picture. I was quickly achieving greater prominence, being recognized for my political involvement.

My visibility did not come without some discouragement, however. In my opinion school district officials were starting to get a little skeptical of me. Mr. Bishop had been informing me that every year my name was the center of discussion at the school board meetings. The issue always was whether I should receive a contract for the next school year. I didn't understand the board's concern because I considered myself to be dedicated to the welfare of the students and, considering that I was not disruptive otherwise, this should have been all that mattered. I was an advocate for education and so was my wife. We had always stressed the importance of education in our household, in the community, and in the teaching profession. There was no way that I should have had a question mark behind my name when it came to receiving a new contract.

The new superintendent who had replaced Dr. Dribben when he retired was Dr. Robert Cagle, a tall militant man from the state of Georgia, formerly a captain in the U. S. Army. Perhaps it was his military background that made him a stickler for observing rules and policy. I never had any disagreements with him and I actually had commended him on his work ethic. I later found out, however, that his conduct had been inappropriate and extreme when it came to dealing with my colleagues. They stated that Dr. Cagle often placed his finger in their faces when he spoke with them and occasionally used rather harsh words in their conversations. I knew he certainly had the disposition to be aggressive if the conversation got heated. I had no reason to have any direct contact with him until I went to question him about a matter that needed addressing.

Dr. Cagle had eliminated a Head Start program that was serving black students successfully at the time. It was the first such program being administered in Greenwood and the director of the program was doing a magnificent job handling it. I didn't understand the problem that led to ending the program; the community had been buoyed from the outset over getting young students into Head Start and now it was abruptly ending without real explanation. One day I left school and decided to go and speak to Dr. Cagle in person concerning the program. At the meeting in his office I merely asked the reason why the program had been cut. He looked piercingly at me and emphatically stated that the decision had been made and that it was final. Dr. Cagle was the type of man who hated to be questioned once he stated his position. I had no choice but to get up and exit his office. We had a Voters' League meeting that night and I found out that Dr. Cagle had had more than his fair share of conflicts with Greenwood people. The complaints I heard about him certainly did not depict him favorably. I had no idea, however, that my own comments about Dr. Cagle's behavior would eventually cause me to be fired from my position as a teacher!

Midnight Train to Georgia

It was a huge disappointment to have programs that were beneficial for African American children eliminated. It appeared that everything that blacks rightfully needed and wanted would not come without a fight. I didn't understand why a program rendering such positive results could possibly be the main focus of opposition when other more pressing issues demanded attention. I was discouraged and furious that Dr. Cagle refused to explain why the Head Start program had been cut. It became even more disturbing to hear about other issues that suffered at his hands from the same kind of irrational and inexplicable reasoning.

Approximately two hundred people showed up at the Voters' League meeting the night we made Dr. Cagle the subject of discussion. I finally said, "Dr. Cagle has gone too far! We will either have to discipline him or put him back on one of those long midnight trains to Georgia!" The crowd just roared in laughter and approval; I went on to say, "The best way to balance the school board is to have two blacks, two whites, and one Chinese." All of my comments made the newspaper headlines, and the news spread around town like a wildfire. There were a few blacks who worked near the superintendent's office who felt I would be fired for my comments, but I didn't believe it. I returned to business as usual believing the sentiment that I expressed was water under the bridge. No one at the school had mentioned anything about the affair, so I focused on the other issues that needed addressing.

The chamber of commerce wanted to meet with the Voters' League to settle our dispute with Dr. Cagle. We met with him around the first of the year in 1979 and I assumed that the year was off to a great start. I felt that our concerns were legitimate and we wanted them addressed. We wanted a black over the band at the high school and there was a science teacher whom we wanted to head the science department. Mr. Robert Wilson was an excellent physics teacher and he also held a master's degree. The white teacher, Mr. Jackson, who was in charge of the program, only held a bachelor's degree. It was obvious that Mr. Wilson was qualified for the position, but for some unexplained reason Dr. Cagle disagreed. I wasn't looking for a confrontation; I was simply looking for people to be rewarded according to what they had earned. It was even more amazing that these black teachers were being overlooked in a majority black school. It wasn't a personal attack on Dr. Cagle; it was merely a fair inquiry as to why blacks were not being hired to head departments. The issues were simply those of fairness and equity. We got into an intense discussion, but we couldn't come to any agreement. I was the most vocal on behalf of blacks and Jimmy Green, president of the county board of supervisors, was the voice for the whites. The white faction claimed that they were going to try and work things out, but I think it was already set in their minds to dismiss me and black people's concerns.

As the month of March 1979 approached, things were relatively quiet for the most part. The principal, Mr. Jackson, and I still had a great relationship. One day he had to be away from the school for a short period of time. He informed the faculty that I would be in charge during his absence. Everybody had gotten accustomed to my being placed in his position while he was away, so it was nothing out of the ordinary. Occasionally a serious matter occurred that I had to handle, as it did this time in the principal's absence. The school had a student teacher from Mississippi Valley State University who taught P.E. One day there were two white students who got into a skirmish during class and he brought them to the office. A white teacher and the P.E. teacher were in the office to observe everything that was transpiring. I spoke with the boys and then administered corporal punishment, giving them five swats each, which was school policy for their misbehavior. It appeared to be no big deal to the boys because they left the office snickering.

It was a week later and I had to go and see the police commissioner about an issue affecting the neighborhood. We had a heated debate over the issue before I left his office for home. A couple of days thereafter I was en route to church for a revival. During the drive I noticed a squad car cruising behind me. The officer pulled me over and asked me to get into the squad car. We drove around the block while he told me about criminal charges that had been leveled against me. I thought that he was mistaken until he told me that the charges came from the mother of one of the boys I had disciplined. I was stunned because this was definitely news to me. I thanked him for the information, but I still couldn't believe it. The next morning I decided to walk to school. I walked past a squad car parked out in front of the school, but I didn't give it much thought. I wasn't able to step foot into my classroom before I was being called on the intercom to report to the office. I walked inside the office and immediately noticed the chief of police sitting there. I sat down. He looked at me and asked if I remembered whipping a little boy about two weeks prior. I replied yes, and immediately asked what the problem was. The chief of police informed me that the mother of one of the boys had filed charges against me. I sat straight up and listened closely to what he was saying and then I was dismissed to return to my class

A few hours later the boy's mother showed up at the school and I was called back into the office. The woman was crying and claiming that I had put blisters on her boy. She went on to fabricate the story more, claiming that the boy could not sleep at night because of the punishment. I was completely stunned by the accusations because I had witnessed with my own eyes the boy playing football and it didn't appear that anything was bothering him. The principal then picked up the telephone and told the chief of police that he would bring me down to the station. I was released almost immediately on a two-hundred-dollar bond and I continued the routine of a normal day. The event, however, quickly captured the attention of the press; the newspaper headlines read, "JORDAN ARRESTED FOR WHIPPING A WHITE CHILD!" The black community was outraged because they knew that I had followed school board policy in my actions. The city attorney questioned me and I informed him that I felt my actions were routine school business. The legal service attorneys were anxious to come to my defense if I had a fight on my hands.

There were at least five hundred angry black folks in the courtroom when my hearing began. In fact, there were so many people present that I thought I would not be able to find a seat, even though I was the one due to testify. When court officials saw and heard all the commotion in the courtroom on my behalf, the prosecuting attorney made a motion to dismiss all charges. I remember clearly how he said, "Just take David Jordan out of here!" I was quite relieved because I knew that I had done nothing wrong. I was sure that things would soon be back to normal. I was wrong. Approximately two weeks later the assistant superintendent walked past my classroom; he spoke and continued down the hallway en route to the principal's office. Five minutes later I was being called to the office. I had no idea what they wanted with me now because things had been rather quiet since the hearing. I could sense something was wrong as soon as I stepped inside the office.

I have never forgotten the words that I heard in the office that day. I wouldn't be receiving a contract for the 1979–1980 school year, which meant that I was being fired as a teacher. I was dumbfounded and immediately looked to Mr. Jackson for an explanation. He was extremely quiet, so I asked him if he was responsible for my losing my job. He quickly went on the defense and reassured me that he had in fact recommended me for another school term. I finally came to learn that Dr. Cagle was responsible for my termination; I was told that I had the right to request a hearing regarding the matter. I'll never forget that feeling as I walked home Friday afternoon after receiving the news. I had so many emotions stirring inside of me, but none greater than sadness. I knew I had to get a grip on things and pull myself together. The next day I was due in Jackson for a state Democratic Executive Committee meeting and I couldn't show how distressed I was. The news hit the press on Sunday, the article making it clear that I was not recommended for a new contract. The community thought I was fired for disciplining the boy, but that was not the reason for my termination. I was fired because of my challenge to the superintendent, boldly exemplified in the comment exclaiming that he should catch the next train smoking back to Georgia!

My hearing against the school board took place in early May at the Education Building downtown. I had a large number of supporters present and among the people there was a representative of the National Education Association. When I arrived at the hearing on that Monday evening, there was a line outside the door. There were people who did not have chairs to sit in, so they squatted on the floor. The gathering was definitely sending a message that I had their full support. I could hear voices saying, "You're not going to do anything to Mr. Jordan!" We stayed this first night until the wee hours of the morning. I found out by the second night that Mr. Bishop had deceived us and that he had actually voted to have me dismissed. I couldn't believe that the man whom the Voters' League had placed on the school board was now supporting the other board members to have me unemployed. I have to admit that it was very disappointing to be double-crossed by someone whom I once held in such high regard. Mr. Bishop attempted to justify his actions by telling people that I needed to shut my mouth.

We also found out during the hearing that the chamber of commerce had validated the board's decision to fire me. They felt that if the superintendent couldn't control one teacher then he wouldn't be able to control four hundred faculty members and staff. The final evening of the hearing was when Mrs. Cornelia Dillard insisted on being present. Mrs. Dillard was an elderly woman, a retired teacher and also the secretary of the Voters' League. She sat in a chair for hours and gave me her full support. I was touched to see how many people actually cared about the future of David Jordan. There were people there who had to walk a great distance to attend the hearing, but they did so to support me. When we wrapped things up I was told that a decision would be reached within ten days. It took only five days before a letter was delivered to me at school. I was once again called to the office and there stood Mr. Whitney Wilson, assistant superintendent, and Mr. Harry Robinson, a black man who administered the district's special education program. Mr. Robinson handed me the letter explaining to me why I was fired. It was a unanimous decision from the school board to dismiss me. I would complete the rest of the school year, but after that I would be considered unemployed.

The school year ended and I faced an uncertain future. I cleaned out my desk drawers and expressed to my colleagues my gratitude of having worked with them. A few of the staff members were noticeably moved to tears over my dismissal. The whole town was actually disturbed and a few individuals wrote letters to the school board in hopes of saving my job. It had been all over the news that David Jordan had been fired! It was a pretty sad and distressing occasion because I knew that I had not done anything to warrant this action. There was even a committee that went to the superintendent's office to get to the root of my termination.

Chris was one of the people who went to the central office because no one wanted an explanation more than she did. She was quite bitter over the injustice that I suffered and she couldn't restrain from calling Dr. Cagle "a dirty dog." She had to be calmed down by the other people who had accompanied her there. When Chris came home, I found out from her that Dr. Cagle had absolutely no explanation to justify my termination. Everybody was angry because I was the voice of the black community and they believed in me. My bold and energetic spirit had gained me an enormous amount of respect in the community. A spate of events followed my dismissal.

I was even put off the deacon's board at my church because I dared speak up in behalf of a musician who was being mistreated. The pastor led the charge in encouraging the members to dismiss me. I refused to allow anyone to run me away from the church, however. I just moved over to the side; I had challenges everywhere else, it seemed, so I looked at this church issue as just another stumbling block to overcome. The last piece of truly disturbing news for that week was a letter from the Ku Klux Klan. Not surprising, given the nature and history of this group, the letter informed me that my activities in the community were being monitored.

Clearly, I was a rejected and dejected man. Understandably, Chris was extremely disappointed with the way things were going against me. I felt down and out, but deep down inside I knew that I had to keep moving. I was eventually offered a full-time position by Dr. Ernest Boykin, president of Mississippi Valley State University if I didn't get my job back in Greenwood. But I told my attorney that I didn't want to go anywhere else for employment. I was born in Leflore County and went to school in Greenwood and I couldn't allow someone from Georgia, a true outsider, to run me away from my very foundation. I had been fighting for everything and everybody else and it was understood that I wanted my job back at all costs, so the real fight for it began.

In the meantime, I thought I should focus some of my attention elsewhere while awaiting the legal outcome of my future employment options. I soon qualified to run for the Mississippi House of Representatives, but I lost by thirty-five votes and thereafter turned my full attention back on my school employment problem. I went to court over the summer to sue for a return to my old job and fifty thousand dollars in damages.

The case went before a federal judge, William C. Keady. I had been before him so many times on other federal cases that he was quite familiar with me. He actually wrote a letter asserting that I had become a professional witness in his courtroom. When he wrote his book *All Rise,* he included my case in the contents. His book was the memoirs of a Mississippi federal judge. It was an honor that we had an opportunity to have him as a guest at the Voters' League before he passed away.

Judge Keady was the kind of jurist who listened carefully to both sides before he rendered a decision. From the start I was optimistic of a fair hearing in his court. He told the school board not to fill my position immediately and that he would have a decision on the case in three weeks. I didn't know how things were going to turn out, but I liked the idea of the judge leaving my position open. It gave me a glimmer of hope as I waited on the determination of my fate. When that time arrived, Judge Keady ruled that I must be reinstated in the classroom. The fact was that I couldn't be fired for expressing my freedom of speech because that violated my First Amendment rights. I spoke my opinions, even the disparaging remark about the superintendent returning to Georgia; I had spoken at the Voters' League meeting and not on school grounds. It was clearly a case of my being punished because I couldn't be controlled and was not easily intimidated. I had requested all my money in a lump sum, but unfortunately this was denied.

Once the decision was handed down, the news immediately hit the press. On the front page of the newspaper was a picture of me standing in the middle of Dr. Cagle and Judge Keady. It appeared that David Jordan had claimed another victory by just standing my ground and not accepting unfair treatment. The school board, however, wasn't satisfied with the decision to rehire me in my old position. They appealed to the Fifth Circuit Court in New Orleans and there three judges upheld Judge Keady's ruling. Their next step was to appeal the case to the U.S. Supreme Court. The school board had already spent over one hundred thousand dollars trying to get rid of me, certainly a wasteful expenditure of limited resources. I knew this money could be better used toward something else, perhaps the reestablishment of the Head Start program. The taxpayers weren't too pleased either and it wasn't long before the press began to editorialize about the school board's fight with me. The newspaper articles continued to imply that the school board was wasting money, and that Dr. Cagle and I needed to resolve our issues. The school board eventually dropped the case and it never got to the Supreme Court. I received a regular teaching contract like the other faculty members, and I looked forward to returning to the classroom.

Chris and I walked into the auditorium on the first day of school and immediately gained everyone's attention. Dr. Cagle was at the podium speaking about new regulations and policies for the school year. The janitors and cafeteria workers were the only ones that openly embraced and welcomed me back. The teachers were quite fearful of interacting with me because they had no idea of what the consequences might be from Dr. Cagle. They had witnessed first-hand that he had no problem with unfairly terminating a teacher. I understood their fear, but I couldn't allow myself to be intimidated by his previous actions.

There was finally a ten-minute break during the assembly and Dr. Cagle used that time to come and shake my hand. He said, "Mr. Jordan, we need to work together." I expressed to him that I had absolutely no problem with us working together. We talked for a brief moment and I believe we were both determined to leave our feud in the past where it belonged. I respected him and his position and I was confident that this battle had earned me his respect. When the meeting was over, I lingered in the auditorium and the teachers immediately came to embrace me. I guess they felt it was now safe since they had seen Dr. Cagle and me bury the hatchet. It took no time for me to focus on the upcoming school year. But I was still quite fascinated with the political arena and I knew it was only a matter of time before I landed myself an elective political office.

My First Political Seat

With the recent court decision in my favor, things were starting to take a more positive turn in my life in 1980. I was ecstatic that Dr. Cagle and I had made a commitment to work together in continuing to educate and promote the students in the Greenwood school system. The Voters' League was getting stronger under my leadership and we were moving to bring greater justice to the people of Greenwood and Leflore County. The league was suing the city seeking a new, more representative form of government and we were waiting for a decision to come down, though we knew that these kinds of case decisions were never resolved quickly. In the meantime, candidates for political office made a constant stream of invited appearances to speak before the league membership. From a practical political perspective, the league and blacks in general in Leflore County were greatly encouraged over the creation of a second congressional district in the state with a majority minority voting percentage. Hence the prospect of the Delta getting its first black congressman looked great. The first black man elected to the state legislature since Reconstruction, Robert Clark, was running for U.S. Congress. I had already decided to run for Congress myself as an independent if a black Democrat didn't win the party nomination. Clark, a humble and well-liked Delta political leader, won, so there was no need for me to run. However, he lost to a Republican in the November election.

In 1976 I had become a part of the New Democrats on the state committee along with fifteen other blacks. The party had come together under one head for the first time since before the civil rights struggle. We had unified racially and abandoned the cochairmanship system to elect President Carter. When Carter was elected, the two racial groups had showed we could work well together in the new direction the state party was taking. This was becoming even more evident in the decade of the 1980s and it proved beneficial for me in many ways. I was getting stronger politically, elevated largely from my leadership role in the Voters' League.

Virtually every political figure on the state level came to the Voters' League for our support and this allowed me to forge tremendous political and personal ties with often very powerful people. We had the governor, secretary of state, state treasurer, and state legislators all coming to get endorsements. State senator Corbet Patridge, whom I knew well, represented Leflore and Sunflower counties at the time. Eventually, after redistricting in 1992, I replaced him in the state senate. Every spring some of us visited the legislature and I would always go to Governor Cliff Finch's office. I knew him quite well. I would take only positive-minded people with me and through a gesture of kindness he would honor them by letting them see how it felt to be a governor for a day. It was a big deal for one of these senior citizens who accompanied me to be able to relax in the governor's chair. The seniors frequently followed me because I was a young energetic schoolteacher and also president of the prestigious and powerful Voters' League. They enjoyed traveling to the state capital and it gave them something to boast about at the next meeting.

After his governorship, Finch lost the election for U.S. Senate to Republican Thad Cochran. Another candidate had been in the senatorial race and this was black Mississippi political icon Charles Evers, the older brother of the slain civil rights leader, Medgar. I will never forget the rally that we held in front of the courthouse to support Charles. At the rally I got an opportunity to meet and introduce the NBA legend Bill Russell, who was in attendance to support Evers, a personal friend. It was a big deal for me because at the time I had never met any sports figure as famous as Russell, a true modern-day basketball giant. I introduced him and he then introduced Charles.

It was during the rally that we noticed Bryon De La Beckwith at the end of the street observing the festivities. He was hesitant about getting too close to the crowd, but everybody recognized him. The African Americans were still angry because we all knew that he was responsible for the death of Medgar Evers. We were there listening to the brother of the man that he had killed. It was just amazing to me that he had the audacity to be in the vicinity knowing that it would stir up bitter feelings. He was still able to walk freely around town and for many that left a bitter taste in their mouths.

The Voters' League hosted our annual banquet and Senator Cochran announced that he recommended to the president of the United States the appointment of the first black federal judge. It was Judge Henry Wingate, who became the first black federal judge ever in the state of Mississippi. He was a guest speaker at the Voters' League and everyone was quite thrilled to have him present. The Voters' League had already become the most active political organization in Mississippi. If there was a problem that arose, people came to the Voters' League seeking help and we immediately looked into it. Moreover, we wanted African Americans not to feel inferior and to seek political positions that had always been reserved for whites.

We realized that the power of the vote was crucial in changing things for the betterment of all people. Hence, the League worked to increase the black vote. I brought approximately seventy-five students from Mississippi Valley State University to register them to vote. But many of the students from the university were from other areas of Mississippi and weren't allowed to register in Leflore County. I gathered some of the students together and we sued the circuit clerk's office in Greenwood. The case went to federal court and I testified on their behalf. The judge ruled that the students would be allowed to vote and we were then permitted to register them. I considered this another major Voters' League and personal accomplishment; young people needed to be encouraged to vote because it was their right and they needed to realize that their vote made a difference.

At this point we had gotten African Americans appointed to most boards in the city and county governments. Moreover, we pushed to encourage blacks to seek elective office at every level. The first African American county supervisor ever elected in Leflore County was Alex Sanders and we were instrumental in his successful campaign. In 1983 I felt it was time for me to run for a political office so I became a candidate for the state senate. I ran as an independent and I was the only African American on the ballot. I thought I had just as good a chance of winning as anyone else considering the district's population was 53 percent black. However, the white people were determined not to see me get into office and they all lined up behind one white candidate. An article in the local newspaper read, "JORDAN WILL WIN THE ELECTION UNLESS . . ." It basically detailed to whites what it would require to keep me out of office. There were even a few black people whom they were able to convince not to vote for me. To be sure, I still had a large number of blacks who supported me, but I lost the election.

In 1984 Mike Espy became the first black Mississippi congressman since Reconstruction. Blacks were elated over his victory; I was especially happy because Mike and I were good friends. He would come by during the campaign and we would discuss his strategy for the election. I assured him that he had the league's full support and he did. He stayed in office for over twelve years until he moved into the position of secretary of agriculture. He would come back to the Voters' League each year to our annual banquet as a guest speaker and give us a congressional report.

In 1985 the courts ruled in our favor for the new form of city government in Greenwood. We could now establish a mayor-council form of government. I seized the moment because this had been a decision that we were confident would be ruled in our favor. It took a few years, but we felt good knowing that justice had been served.

It was now time for me to take a shot at running for another political seat. I ran for a local office and became the first black person elected to the Greenwood City Council. I had three opponents in the Democratic Party primary and I defeated all three of them. It was an exciting time because during the campaign NBC came to Greenwood and I received an opportunity to be filmed and seen on national television. They were there to cover a story of the thirty-year anniversary of the Emmett Till case. To the people who knew the details surrounding the case, it was like it happened yesterday. African Americans from the Mississippi Delta never did get over the fact that Emmett Till's killers got away with cold-blooded murder. I knew it was even more difficult for Till's mother to forget the images of her son's distorted body and this probably haunted her for decades. She was still seeking justice for his death. I supported the idea of never allowing the world to forget the death of Emmett Till. When NBC came to Greenwood, they filmed me speaking at a rally. The film was shown on the *Morning Show* with Bryant Gumbel after I won the election. It was televised all over the nation and it was another defining moment in the beginning of my political career.

I was still teaching and was now a city council member. Many people didn't like the fact that I was a city councilman. Their argument was that I shouldn't be allowed to teach in the Greenwood public school system and also hold office as a city council member. Some of these people, among them my bitterest critics, wanted me to resign from the city government. They filed ethics charges against me stating that it was unlawful for me to be on a city council that approves the school budget. The city council was responsible for appointing the school board, which makes the school budget with the approval of the city council. The critics sought to distort the issue, arguing that my dual status meant I was my own boss—that I could set my teaching salary to whatever I wanted it to be. All of this, they claimed, violated the Mississippi Constitution. But it was ridiculous logic, just simply untrue. The state ethics commission ruled in my favor, maintaining that I had not violated Section 109 of the Mississippi Constitution. This provision states that an official can't serve in a capacity that benefits him or her more than it does any other person. I had a master's degree in science and years of teaching experience, but I wasn't earning any more salary than anyone else with the same qualifications. I stayed on the city council and I continued to teach. I did receive a list of the people who had filed against me. They were not constituents from my district, but people who lived in North Greenwood, all of them white. Moreover, there were some names on the list that completely shocked me. These people definitely didn't want me to serve on the city council. I believe the major reason was because I had a well-known history of initiating and participating in successful lawsuits. I had sued the city to change the form of government; I had sued the school district and the second congressional district. I had testified in a lot of cases in federal court. I now held a political office and for some, this was entirely too much power for a black man in Greenwood at the time.

We were sworn in right after the Fourth of July holiday. There were four Democrats and three Republicans, but only three were African American. Once we were sworn in, we got our first black city prosecuting attorney in Greenwood. We didn't get as much as we wanted, because I wanted to see a black city clerk, but our effort only received three favorable votes. With just three black votes we succeeded in getting only a few perks, but I knew we could get much more if we continued to stick together.

Our campaign for a federal holiday honoring Dr. Martin Luther King Jr. began right after his assassination. It wasn't until 1983 that President Ronald Reagan signed the national holiday into law and it was first observed on January 20, 1986. The bill first came to vote in 1979, but it fell five votes short of the number needed for passage. There were two major arguments why Congress refused to pass the bill. The first was that a paid holiday for federal employees would be too expensive for the government. The other reason was that a paid holiday to honor a private citizen would be contrary to long-standing tradition of not recognizing someone like King who had never held public office. There were only two other people who had national holidays honoring them and they were George Washington and Christopher Columbus. Even after the King holiday measure passed some states resisted observing it as such by giving it alternative names or combining it with other holidays. Indeed, President Reagan even opposed the holiday initially, but Congress had passed it with an overwhelming veto-proof majority. It wasn't officially observed in all fifty states until 2000. This effort took a long time, but supporters never wavered in the cause and because of this I was personally validated in my belief that persistence usually paid off. I was overwhelmed with joy to see an African American man honored by having a national holiday in his name. It was a great way to honor his life and legacy, an excellent way to educate future generations about such a great and powerful leader.

In the following year, 1987, there was an attack made on my home. State senator Doug Anderson of Jackson and I led a march, along with four hundred people, honoring Dr. Martin Luther King Jr. We marched down Martin Luther King Drive in Greenwood on January 18 in observance of King's birthday. It was later that night that a brick, along with a typed note from the Ku Klux Klan, was thrown through my car's rear window. The note read as follows: "As a citizen of this town you have continued to cause trouble among the blacks and whites. If you proceed to urge the recognition of Martin Luther King Jr. there will be aggressive action taken on behalf of the white citizen. What you have witnessed thus far is only a small occurrence of what will happen if you don't discontinue your strive for racial equality. A 'nigger' like yourself will never be equal to the white race. We have been watching you for some time now and we have now begun our quest for your removal from this city. Remove yourself from further activity in this town. It would be a shame if we had to waste another day and recognize your birthday." The note didn't change my attitude about doing things that are right, but it bothered me that I had been under personal attack ever since I became president of the Voters' League. I felt the town belonged to everyone, blacks and whites, and it was my constitutional right to support the cause of honoring my hero and the hero of countless other Americans. It was painful to see that racial discrimination was still very much in existence.

The attack made all the local newspapers and shortly thereafter even made *Jet* magazine. The damage to my 1985 Oldsmobile was estimated at about a thousand dollars. The FBI immediately began investigating the incident. I went to school the next day an hour later than my scheduled time. The whole school, students and faculty, had heard about the incident and they all expressed genuine concerns about the safety of me and my family. It was an eerie feeling, not knowing who was watching me or my home, but I refused to allow anyone to run me out of town. My fight for justice wasn't for personal gain; it was to make sure that African Americans received the same opportunities that were given to white people. I didn't see anything wrong with what I was doing and I had come too far to turn back now anyway.

In 1989 I became the president of the city council. Blacks were also now the majority vote with four on the board. On my agenda next was to get a black city clerk and a black fire chief appointed. Although a black assistant fire chief was hired in 1988, a real achievement for black Greenwood aspirations, I didn't see why we couldn't have a black fire chief. This too I saw as justice. I recommended a lady by the name of Deidra Mays for the position of city clerk. She had a master's degree in accounting from Mississippi Valley State University and she was well qualified for the position. The mayor refused to appoint her and we went a whole year with an assistant city clerk handling the leadership duties. We had to vote on any candidate for the appointment and the black councilmen refused to support anyone else until we got what we wanted. The mayor finally gave in and hired the lady of our choice and she remained the city clerk for at least eighteen years. Mrs. Mays was the best city clerk that Greenwood ever had and the city certainly prospered from her expertise. We got the black city clerk whom we wanted and the black fire chief at the same time. I was immediately blamed for everything that some people didn't want to see happen. The white opposition that held me responsible began filing ethics charges against me again and again, but the charges never stuck.

Following our recent success our next task was to get a black city attorney appointed. The mayor's assertion that he had the power to appoint the attorney was correct, but only the council had the authority to confirm the designee. It appeared that we had another fight on our hands. We wouldn't confirm the appointment of his choice, so the mayor sued the city council. We went to federal court and the judge ruled in our favor; we got the city attorney we wanted. This was considered another clear-cut victory for black citizens in Greenwood, a huge step in our quest for political justice and equity.

In the midst of all the recent turbulence and political maneuvering surrounding my life I could at least take great solace from the success my children were experiencing. The year 1989 was also the year that Darryl and his wife, Jennifer, both received Meharry Medical College medical degrees. After Darryl received his degree and completed his training, he began his practice in Nashville. Donald was actually the first one to attend Meharry Medical College in Nashville, but he stumbled on some academic difficulties and decided to take a break. He had completed two years before his withdrawal to obtain a job as a chemist in Rockford, Illinois.

Donald worked at the chemical company for about five to six years. I think when Darryl completed medical school it inspired Donald to go back to school. I remember Donald called us and asked if he could come home and go to pharmacy school and of course we didn't hesitate to welcome him back. We were always in full support of our children when it came to their advancement. Darryl eventually returned to Mississippi because he wanted to become a pulmonologist and practice in his home state. It was amazing to me how things had turned out and how much of a blessing had come from frequently dim life situations. Chris and I were at different times struck with tuberculosis and it was during the time that she was pregnant with both boys. The thought of them picking professions in the medical field was amazing and definitely uplifting.

My work in behalf of racial justice had been recognized in a number of places in Mississippi, but now I had begun to achieve national visibility. One of the first places where this recognition occurred was in Chicago, a city I fondly remember first visiting because Morgan Freeman and I were being honored there by a group called the Chicago-Greenwood Culture Club. Former Greenwood residents living in Chicago had organized the club. Morgan was unable to attend the ceremony because he was in Georgia filming the movie *Glory*, so his sister received the award in his absence. These were turning out to be favorable times for me; I was extremely happy about the way things were going in my life and then I was hit with some devastating news!

A Bittersweet Victory

In 1990, I was invited by Congressman Mike Espy to meet Nelson Mandela in Washington, D.C. Chris was in Nashville at the time helping out with the grandchildren and I called her to inform her that she needed to come home. I was extremely excited about meeting Mandela and I wanted Chris to join me. The next day she was on the bus headed back to Mississippi and when she arrived we jumped in the car and drove to Washington. We had been watching the news about the Africans suffering in South Africa. It was extremely disturbing to see them being whipped so severely for simply protesting against racial and political injustices. Nelson Mandela had been released from prison in February of 1990, after being incarcerated for twenty-seven years. Mandela had been arrested in 1962 and imprisoned in the Johannesburg Fort. He was charged with leading workers to strike in 1961 and leaving the country illegally. Two years later, while he was imprisoned, he was charged with crimes of sabotage and crimes equivalent to treason. The prosecutor also accused Mandela of plotting a foreign invasion of South Africa, which Mandela emphatically denied. South African followers of Mandela considered him a political prisoner and remained steadfast in advocating his release from prison and their support of his leadership. He became South Africa's first democratically elected president after his release. I had heard so much about him and I had a tremendous amount of respect for this man, a hero to many people worldwide. He had indeed endured and overcome a tremendous amount of struggle. I couldn't imagine missing the opportunity to shake hands with a man for whom I had so much admiration.

Chris and I stopped in Atlanta en route to Washington, D.C. In

Atlanta a documentary was in production on Emmett Till and the producers wanted to interview me. I was a little disappointed to discover that there were young African Americans from Chicago who had never heard of Emmett Till. I knew there was still work to be done to educate our people on historical figures and issues that had had a significant impact on our history.

We finally arrived at our destination and were introduced to Nelson Mandela. I shook hands with him and was quite impressed with his wife, Winnie. They appeared to be a perfect couple and I found her extremely charming. She had a heavy British accent and she was quite impressive with the way she carried herself. Winnie was much younger than Nelson and perhaps that is the reason for their eventual divorce, but I was quite disappointed when they later made the decision to go their separate ways. I also had an opportunity to meet Robert Kennedy's son. The trip was indeed an experience that Chris and I will never forget and I was glad to be part of such a historical event.

In January of 1991 I took a trip to Toledo, Ohio, to visit my brother Andrew, who had become quite ill. I wanted to spend quality time with him because our bond as brothers had always been close. Sister had been in contact with him and his conversation led her to believe that Andrew felt that his time was near. Andrew spoke of a strong desire to come home and see Momma and Poppa. We realized later that he wasn't referring to the home in Mississippi, but the place with our heavenly father. I wanted and needed to see my brother because it appeared that he was sounding weaker each time we spoke. I was truly surprised and distressed when Andrew personally picked me up from the bus station. I couldn't believe how much weight he had lost. He was suffering from colon cancer and I was deeply saddened by what the affliction had actually done to him. We drove past the cemetery where Clevester was buried and I could see the distress in Andrew's eyes. If ever there was a time that I wished I could change the course of something it was now. I had been in many battles, but I knew none compared to the fight that my brother was encountering to stay alive. We sat around reflecting on all the wonderful memories that we had created and shared throughout the years. My brother had been such a major part of my life, definitely a great friend over the years. I remember staring out the window at the ice and snow on the ground as we reminisced about our lives. The coldness and darkness on the outside symbolized the pain that now weighed so heavily on my heart. We could no longer hold back the tears because the reality was that we both knew that this would probably be the last time that we bonded as brothers.

I returned home and broke the news to Chris about the devastating circumstances surrounding Andrew's health. We called and encouraged him to increase his diet, but he didn't have an appetite. I loved my brother, but God loved him best and ended his suffering on March 16, 1991. We gathered as a family and headed to Toledo, Ohio, to put my brother to rest. I delivered the eulogy at his service, a very sad occasion for me. Andrew had also been committed to making a difference in the way African Americans were treated. He had been a dedicated teacher in the Toledo school district. His daughter later wrote a book about his life and acknowledged his participation in the civil rights movement. Andrew's death was quite devastating to me, but I knew my brother would want me to continue my fight for racial justice. That same year Chris and Viola decided that it was time to retire from teaching. They wanted to enjoy their golden years and spend time with the grandchildren. I was planning my retirement for the following year, so it was time for me to begin preparing for the next step in my life.

The Black Caucus of the Mississippi legislature began to draw up new districts. The population of African Americans had increased to an extent that we could have more representation in the legislature. Caucus leaders tried to find civil rights activists as potential candidates and to establish legislative districts in which they had a chance to be victorious. My good friend Senator Doug Anderson wanted to draw a line in such a way for me to have an opportunity to run for the senate. I had a lot of unused vacation days on the books that I needed to use before I made a decision to retire. I would leave school around noon on many occasions and drive to Jackson to work with the Black Caucus on drawing up the redistricting plan. We worked closely with long-time black Mississippi political activist Henry Kirksey, an expert in drawing up majority black districts. The new district map included my precinct in Greenwood.

In January of 1992 I announced that I would run for a senate seat in the Mississippi legislature. All of my white critics in Greenwood were certainly happy because if I was elected they concluded that they would not have to contend with me any more on the city council. Some black supporters volunteered to help me campaign. After the lines were finalized, I qualified to run as a Democrat in the August primary in the newly created District 24. All of this occurred during the time that Bill Clinton announced his candidacy for president of the United States. I immediately began campaign plans for the region carved out for me. The district included Holmes, Leflore, and Tallahatchie counties. I started campaigning in Holmes County, and found out I was already very well known there. I had also taught in the Holmes County school district during the 1969–1970 school year and many people, I'm sure, still remembered me from this experience. The campaign was off to a decent start because it appeared that people actually wanted to see me in the senate. They wanted me in the legislature mainly because of my civil rights record. I was also known for my leadership role in the Voters' League. My grandson Larry Dugar Jr. even visited from New Orleans to help me campaign during the summer. As time passed there were other candidates qualifying to run in the election. A young white attorney from Holmes County decided to run against me and he actually got some support from many African Americans.

The primary was scheduled for August, occurring in the midst of the Democratic National Convention. I was invited to New York to attend the convention and Chris accompanied me. She had not been on many long plane rides and preparation for the New York flight made her a little more nervous than usual. She began leaving instructions with the children as if we would not be returning home and this, in turn, began to make me feel a little uneasy. Apprehension aside, we eventually boarded the same flight with members of the Mississippi media headed to New York.

We arrived safely in New York City. The convention was held in Madison Square Garden, where former heavyweight boxing champion Joe Louis had held most of his title fights. While in New York I contacted a group that wanted an opportunity to visit Mississippi. The group was dedicated to campaigning for the Democratic Party and registering young people to vote. I was extremely impressed by what they represented and I was more than willing to assist them. We stayed in New York a total of six days. I had never before been in a city quite as crowded. It seemed that with every step I took I saw a bunch of yellow taxicabs and everywhere I turned I saw a mass of people. I was actually ready to get back to the South and at least be able to see the earth instead of so much asphalt and concrete. It was a great experience to be able to visit other cities, but there was still no place like home.

When we returned home, a young man from the group that I met in New York came to visit, along with about thirty other people. He stayed in our home and Chris cooked him some fried chicken, sweet potatoes, black-eyed peas, turnip greens, and cornbread. The other people stayed at the National Guard Armory facility and slept in sleeping bags. I paid Mississippi Valley State University close to four hundred dollars to feed them during their stay. We immediately started canvassing the black community to be sure they exercised their right to vote. We were filmed about the process that we took to make people aware of the upcoming election. I discussed in the film information about Greenwood being the home of Medgar Evers's killer. There was also mention of my state senate candidacy and this made the national news.

A week later, in the Democratic primary, I defeated the white attorney by 70 percent of the votes. We were elated that I had won the party nomination for state senate. Now it was forward to an even more arduous contest. In the general election, I had two opponents and they were both white males; one was an independent candidate and the other a Republican. Everyone around me felt confident that I would be victorious in the election. I remember that one of my opponents claimed that he didn't know that I was that qualified despite my landslide victory in the primary. I had built a good reputation through the Voters' League. We had the pleasure of having some great elected politicians speak before our organization. I was now seeking votes to hold a political office and I received support from places that I never imagined I would. I made speeches virtually everywhere and did everything politically possible to assure myself a victory when November arrived. I won the general election by 72 percent of the votes. It was a major accomplishment to have reached a point in my life where I was now a state senator. There is only one thing that could have made the victory sweeter and that is if my deceased family members could have been around to witness it.

It wasn't long after I won the election that I began to get phone calls from the newspaper inquiring about my resignation from the city council. I couldn't help but chuckle because I realized how badly some people wanted me removed from the council. I explained to them that my position would not go into effect until January of the following year and that was when I planned to resign. I had already retired from teaching in May of 1992, but I was still president of the city council. I took the position after the president, Dr. Joseph Curtis, passed away, and I planned on serving for only two years. Dr. Curtis was also a professor at Mississippi Valley State University. I was the one with the experience and expertise, which qualified me to step smoothly into his position. It didn't matter what my qualifications were to my harshest critics in Greenwood because the bottom line was they wanted me out of city government. I wouldn't receive any pay for my position as senator until after the first of the year. The press immediately informed the state attorney general that I had won the senate seat and had not yet resigned from the city council. The attorney general gave them the most shocking news when he told me that I didn't have to resign unless I wanted to. The reason, he said, was because I was a legislator as a city councilman and I was a legislator in the state senate. This did not violate the laws of separation of power involving the three judicial branches of government. These were the legislative, the executive, and the judicial and I was consistent in my capacity because I was a legislator in both city and state government. My white adversaries were definitely not satisfied with that explanation and they decided to appeal to the state ethics commission. They received the same results that they had gotten from the attorney general's office. I decided that since my dual office-holding was such a big deal to some of these people that I was going to have fun with the issue. I resolved that I would hold both offices and see what came of it. It was January of 1993 when I took my oath and began serving in the state senate. I was commuting between Jackson and Greenwood to make sure that I attended the city council meetings and fulfilled my obligation in the senate. It was a routine that I became accustomed to and it lasted the whole legislative session.

One day I was leaving the senate chambers and a reporter approached me. He said, "Senator Jordan, did you know that they have introduced a bill in the house of representatives to remove you from being a city councilman?" I was astounded to hear what the young man was telling me because I had no knowledge of this. The reporter went on to inform me that one of my fellow colleagues from Leflore County, Representative Jimmy Green, had introduced the bill. I was even more surprised to learn that citizens from Leflore County had asked him to introduce it. The bill passed the house of representatives and then it came to the senate. The senate president assigned the bill to the Election Committee, which passed it out of committee before it came to the senate floor.

I had no idea that my first fight in the senate would be a bill that revolved around me. I had always been the focus of attention because of my strong belief in doing what was fair. All of the battles that I had encountered thus far were fought to make an injustice become a justice. I was once again forced into the limelight because of my respect for the law and commitment to doing the right thing. The senators wanted to know what law I was breaking, but there had been no violations. I hadn't been in office long enough to make any friends or allies in the legislature, so I had to speak on my own behalf. It seemed that the debate wasn't about breaking laws. It was about the fact that I held dual offices and it just didn't look right. One of the senators simply asked the committee chair, "What do we have to do with it?" He added, "Senator Jordan has been elected by the people in his ward for city council and he's been elected to the state senate from the district. It seems apparent that the people want him so what is it that you want us to do?" The simple fact was that they had never known anyone who had held two elected offices. The senators debated the issue for over twenty-four hours. They debated so intensely at one point that it brought tears to Senator Rob Smith's eyes. A few senators believed racism was at the core of the debate. One of them was Senator Joe Clay Hamilton who made this point as he spoke on my behalf. We finally killed the bill in this session, and nothing happened to alter my status in Greenwood, but the following year it was back on the table. There was a different outcome this time as the senate passed the bill. The result, however, had to be cleared by the U.S. Justice Department under the 1965 Voting Rights Act provision because the senate vote constituted a change in voting procedures. I asked for floor privileges to further debate the bill. I simply made one statement: "This isn't the end of this fight! This fight will end in Washington, D.C.!"

Justice Across the Board

The issue of my holding office in both the senate and city council was still very much an unresolved problem. The controversy concerning the bill allowed me an opportunity to meet the United States assistant attorney general, Deval Patrick, who later became the first black elected governor of Massachusetts. The bill addressing my dual offices was presented to him for review. He had someone from his office contact me and a call was also placed to the author of the bill. A young black attorney who had joined Bill Clinton's staff was handling the situation. She was one of the few African American attorneys whom Clinton had worked with while serving as governor of Arkansas. She was also one of the few he took with him when he moved into the presidency. I'll never forget the phone call that I received from her and the anger that came from her voice when we talked. She had tried to negotiate with the author of the bill concerning the issue, but she had been unsuccessful. She felt he had disrespected her in their conversation and said, "He hung up on me and I just wanted you to know that we're not going to preclear this damn bill!" I simply said, "Thank you and I agree with you 100 percent." I received a letter from the U.S. Department of Justice stating what had been forwarded to the state of Mississippi. It appeared that this whole affair was some type of punishment, because I had violated no laws of the state of Mississippi.

As a result of the information placed before Assistant Attorney General Patrick he could not preclear the bill. The bill violated Section 5 of the Voting Rights Act of 1965 and this prevented the bill from becoming law. Patrick's office sent me a letter supporting my argument that the bill was racially motivated. I had won again. I had even been reelected to the council during the time that the bill was being debated. I was pleased that the Justice Department had ruled in my favor, but I wasn't too surprised by the ruling. I knew that in this day in time they couldn't create a law just to affect me because they disagreed with my political views. The fact that someone was holding two political offices might have been contrary to anything that this Mississippi Delta town had ever seen, but this didn't make it illegal and to this present day I've been serving in dual office. It did not matter who disapproved of my positions I have been determined to hold them for as long as the people wanted me.

My first year in the senate was spent learning the process and debating bills. I did not chair any committee, but I was vice-chair of the Bank and Finance Committee. I served on the Municipalities Committee since I was so experienced in city government. I also served on the University and College Committee. I didn't have an office in the capitol because they were assigned by seniority. I did have an office across the street in another building, but I never used it and rarely went into the building.

In 1994 Governor Kirk Fordice wanted to appoint some members to the college board. There were four vacancies and he wanted to appoint all white members to the board. The chairman of the committee was Senator Hillman Frazier. He was an African American and he didn't want to approve the governor's request; he assigned the matter to a subcommittee. The subcommittee included African Americans Alice Hardin, Johnnie Walls, Sampson Jackson, and me. He put us on the committee along with two white senators. Blacks had the majority and we rejected the recommendations because there were no African Americans designated as appointees; neither was there a white female. The governor was furious about our action and immediately began to put pressure on the committee to take deliberations away from the subcommittee. Many Mississippians were angry about the issue and lined up on one side or the other, but we continued to address the matter. I received phone calls accusing me of being a racist and a lot of hate mail denigrating me in the worst way. I continued to explain that my position on the issue was about fairness. There were four vacancies and I suggested the governor appoint a white female and an African American male to two of the openings. When my comments were made public women from the University of Mississippi and others from across the state joined me in the fight.

At the same time of the college board controversy, there was another issue garnering a great deal of my attention. This had to do with the mayor of Greenwood's proposal to hire an attorney whom we could not support because he had sued the city council. The news traveled to the Klan that we were having trouble within the city council. The Klan had sent a letter stating that they would be on the steps of the courthouse protesting their disagreements with the city council. The black councilmen held a meeting to deal with the issues before us. We were advised by many concerned about our safety to stay home on the day that the Klan planned to visit. The mayor gathered the president of Mississippi Valley State University, a few ministers, and some other leaders to join him in finding a way to end the charged atmosphere. They held a prayer vigil at the courthouse in hopes that the Klan would bypass Greenwood. I had made it clear, however, that I would be present at the courthouse when the Klan arrived. I canvassed the city seeking people who would join me at city hall to confront the Klan, and twenty-five people agreed. The mayor called the morning that the Klan was due to arrive and told me that they were not showing up. I hung up the phone and told Chris that I was going to stick to my original plan. I went into the community and gathered the people who had agreed to join me. When the Klan showed up we were already positioned on the steps of the courthouse. I was standing with my pastor, Congressman Bennie Thompson, and Representative Willie Perkins. The Grand Dragon of the Klan stepped right in front of my face, our noses almost touching. I quickly shoved him back and people immediately moved to separate us. I did not like the fact that this man, of all people, was deliberately trying to intimidate me by getting into my breathing space. The news media and reporters were gathered around and the incident made the headlines of the paper. The Grand

Dragon stated that he was going to sue me for aggravated assault. The media supported his allegations, acknowledging that I did put my hands on him. The Klan eventually traveled to Clarksdale where they were arrested. There were a few people who claimed to have been disappointed by my actions. In my answer to them, I simply said, "I had a right to be there because I pay taxes and I was there first. There was no way in hell that I was going to allow the Klan to come to Greenwood and stand on the steps that we were already occupying!" Threats aside, nothing thereafter followed the incident, and the Klan never returned to Greenwood. They didn't speak atop the Greenwood steps and I was glad that we had stood our ground.

There were two special sessions called over the summer to try and get a bill passed that would deny the governor's recommendation to name only white males to the college board vacancies. Black senators turned it down because we specifically wanted a white female and a black male and we were not deviating from our demands. In the second session late one night things began to turn around and we got what we wanted. The governor finally gave in; the new board appointees would consist of two white males, one black male, and one white female. It was our first stand in challenging the governor and we were victorious. But my place on the University and College Committee became a casualty because I was not reappointed when my term on it expired. It didn't bother me because I was gratified with what we had just accomplished and I could bask for some time in the courageous stand that resulted in another victory in achieving equality. Besides, there would be other battles of great significance to fight on other legislative committee battlegrounds.

The year 1994 also witnessed the completion of unfinished business in a case in which justice had been long denied. For over three decades Medgar Evers's killer had escaped punishment for his cowardly and dastardly act. But because of the persistence of Medgar's widow, Myrlie, and Jerry Mitchell, a white reporter for the Jackson *Clarion-Ledger*, the Beckwith trial was reopened. Byron De La Beckwith had already been tried twice for Medgar's murder in 1964 but both trials ended in mistrials. The all-white male juries that served in both cases had twice been unable to reach a verdict. There was evidence from the subsequent investigation that these jurors had been illegally screened. Beckwith would now have to deal with a third trial but with a different set of circumstance in terms of jury composition. This time there would be eight blacks and four whites on the jury. The same physical evidence from the prior trials was used, buttressed by proof that Beckwith had bragged about the murder at a Klan rally and to others at different times since the initial mistrials. I remember the emotionally intense trial that took place in Jackson, Mississippi, and it lasted through most of the legislative session. On February 5, 1994, Byron De La Beckwith was convicted of murder in the first degree. He was sentenced to life in prison without the possibility of parole. The state of Mississippi finally felt that justice had been served and African Americans were elated. I felt great about his conviction and his brother, Charles Evers, understandably was quite happy over the outcome. Charles Evers had stepped into his brother's shoes as field director of the NAACP of Mississippi after Medgar's assassination. Charles also went on to become the first African American mayor in Fayette, Mississippi, and continued his work as a prominent civil rights advocate. There was eventually a movie made about the murder of Medgar Evers and an account of this third trial. Whoopi Goldberg played the role of Myrlie Evers. Goldberg is a very prominent actress and a strong woman.

The following year marked the fortieth anniversary of justice being denied in a different case. It was August of 1955 when one of the most horrific crimes in African American history, indeed in American history, occurred. Despite the obvious guilt of the men tried for this crime, no justice prevailed for Emmett Till and his family. It was, however, the turning point for African Americans in our fight for equality. The anniversary of the death of a child could serve as a painful memory to any mother, but Mamie Till decided to look at her son's death in a spiritual way. In her August 1995 interview published in the *Greenwood Commonwealth,* Mrs. Till discussed how she found the strength to deal with her son's death. She realized that Emmett had been put on this earth for a special assignment and that he would never be forgotten. She couldn't have imagined that her son would be the catalyst for the civil rights movement and spark great leaders to stand up and step forward. After reading her interview and learning of the inspiration to courage that his murder sparked I felt uplifted in knowing that his death was not in vain. The remembrance of Emmett Till's death marks a life-changing event in the consciousness of America and is something that African Americans shall not forget. There is always a wonderful feeling that comes over me when I feel that justice is being served. It might not always happen immediately or without a fight, but whenever it happens it's a victory for righteousness and certainly gratifying.

The year 1995 was also a year that the legislature passed a hefty state budget and we accomplished a lot. We put ten million dollars aside for municipalities to receive small loans at 1 or 2 percent interest rate from the fund. If a small town needed two hundred thousand dollars it could borrow the money at a lower cost than from any other source. The industrial sector in Greenwood was doing well. One of our major plants was the Baldwin Piano Company, which employed about eight hundred people. And there was the Viking Range Company, which employed between five and six hundred people. This was a period when the economy was booming and citizens were doing well. Symbolic of this period of prosperity, legislators often travelled out of state to attend national conferences geared to issues of legislative interests. I took advantage of the opportunities to travel to many other cities. The remarkable part was that Chris could accompany me in seeing various parts of the country where we had never been or spent much time before. I considered those times to be a part of our golden years.

In 1996 Ronnie Musgrove became lieutenant governor and he appointed me chairman of the Municipalities Committee. It was a perfect job for me because I was on the Greenwood City Council with ten years of experience; clearly from a practical political standpoint I knew more about city government than almost all of my colleagues in the state government. I was able to push through meaningful legislation at a quicker pace from my committee position and I acquired many good and powerful friends in the process. There were 298 municipalities in the state of Mississippi and they looked for the chairman of Municipalities in the senate and the house of representatives to get their legislation passed. I was accommodating and had absolutely no problem pushing through the legislation that the Mississippi Municipal League proposed to us if I thought it would benefit the cities. I had a great time in this position and people respected me because they knew I would speak up for what was proper and fair. As a senator I championed legislation that was often very beneficial to the welfare of a specific group of people. For example, at this time many teachers were retiring from the public school system and had a great need for large amounts of money as they made the transition to their new status. The legislature passed a retirement package with a provision that offered teachers the choice to draw a lump sum of the money from their retirement fund and prorate the remaining amount in monthly installments for as long as they lived. The lump sum available to them varied, depending on how long the retiree had taught. Many teachers liked the lump sum feature and the provision allowing them to substitute-teach for four and a half months out of the year without adversely affecting their monthly retirement benefits. Indeed, they could even cross the state line and teach full-time in the bordering states and still draw their full Mississippi retirement. This retirement package was a pretty good deal and it helped to open other doors of opportunities for former teachers, including the chance to become paid elected officials. This ended a feature of Mississippi law that previously allowed former teachers drawing retirement to serve in municipal government, but without pay. Another of the bills that I pushed through allowed employees covered in the retirement fund to draw their full retirement money from the fund before they retired; elected officials covered in the retirement fund were able, if they chose to do so, to draw 25 percent of their annual salary, plus full retirement. I wanted to raise it to as much as 75 percent, but I couldn't get the committee to go along with me on this larger maximum. If a person was making twenty thousand dollars a year as mayor of a small town then he could draw five thousand dollars from his account plus receive his monthly retirement and that made a difference to a lot of people. I held the position of chairman of Municipalities for a total of eight years and in that time period a lot of bills that we needed were passed because I could get the votes. There were many people who were happy having me in this position because as an active councilman myself, I knew the people's needs. The question of my holding dual office slowly faded away.

The Mississippi Adequate Education Program bill was also passed in 1996. This was a program developed in order to assure that every public school district would have adequate revenue to operate. There are 152 public school districts in the state of Mississippi. There was about $135,000,000 put into public education and we were extremely happy about this program. Some school districts in poor counties had barely been able to exist because they didn't have much of a tax base. The Mississippi Adequate Education Program gave each school district a set amount of money from the state to upgrade their system. I played a major part in passage of this program because I served on the senate Education Committee and have been on this committee for the past nineteen years. I was also serving on the Finance Committee, which was really crucial because of the attempt to close Mississippi Valley State University. The plan was to phase Valley State University out gradually, but I fought tooth and nail to make sure that this didn't occur. As a result of my tenacity to insure the college's survival, I received twelve million dollars over a period of time to build a new four-story building, which was the administration building, on the campus. We were able to fight off closure and with me being an alumnus of Valley I had a strong allegiance to do so each time the subject resurfaced. It's been a tough battle to keep Valley open and to provide the resources for the school to function on its highest level, but I will continue to fight.

I have always considered myself a furious debater when it involved issues concerning African Americans. I also have had a strong commitment to fighting for the underdog. I remember there was a group of people called "loggers" who lived up in the hills. They were white men who made their living cutting timber and providing wood for the paper mill. An issue surfaced claiming that they were being cheated because their work was being measured incorrectly. They got into their trucks and rode around the capitol in protest, blowing their horns in an attempt to get the legislators' attention. They wanted laws passed that would benefit loggers. I found it rather interesting how they attempted to draw attention to their plight and the need for legal remedy. Their senators would go to the podium in support of their cause arguing for the appropriate legislation, but they would get voted down, the bill defeated. I started thinking about how African Americans were often mistreated and I realized that everyone deserved to be treated fairly; I took the podium on their behalf. I debated and fought for them with like-minded colleagues until we eventually got a bill passed to benefit the loggers. I gained a lot of additional support because I championed their cause; I felt that their civil rights were being violated and the loggers appreciated my taking a stand for them.

I have written numerous bills dealing with education issues, but none more important than the Character Education Bill. The program became effective in the 1999–2000 school year and I was quite proud to be the author of this bill. I felt that since children spent a tremendous amount of time in the classroom the school districts should assist in helping to develop students' character traits. This bill would not only be effective in the classroom, but in everyday life. The program affected students from grades K–12. The character traits we sought to influence included "courage, patriotism, citizenship, honesty, pride in quality work, fairness, respect for and obedience to the law, respect for others, kindness, cooperation, self-respect, self-control, courtesy, compassion, diligence, generosity, punctuality, cleanliness, cheerfulness, school pride, respect for the environment, patience, creativity, sportsmanship, loyalty, and perseverance." The law is still in effect today and children have benefited tremendously from the goals of the program. I always believed that nothing beats failure but a try. We must not give up on implementing new programs that will give our children the tools necessary to compete in today's society. The recognition I gained from bills of this nature added to my credibility among many people, including former critics, but there were many more bills to pass!

Allegiance to the Flag

In 1999 as the world was getting prepared for the twenty-first century I remained steadfast and passionate about the role I was playing politically in Mississippi. I still served as chairman of Municipalities and pushed forward a lot of legislation through this committee that was beneficial for cities in the state. At the same time I continued serving on the city council in Greenwood and as president of the Voters' League. My work in Greenwood kept me tremendously busy but close to home and family. I was fortunate to have the competent assistance of colleague Robert Sims as vice president of the Voters' League; he filled in for me when duties in Jackson required me to be there. The times when I was able to attend the meetings at the Voters' League I would often bring a few of my legislative colleagues with me from Jackson. We would return to the capital that night after the meeting ended. I made sure that the African American senators especially made remarks during the Voters' League meetings. I thought it was good politics and I also wanted the local people to see and meet other black senators from the legislature.

This was also a disappointing time for the Democratic Party because President Clinton's final term was ending. The president had done an excellent job of running the country. He got the country out of debt, balanced the budget and created a surplus of more than a trillion dollars. He was great in growing the economy—his policies created jobs and established a period of notable prosperity for the nation. Black Americans loved him and made great strides during his administration. He just knew how to make things work for the betterment of all the American people. Clinton was a southerner who didn't receive much support from the Republican Party, but that didn't adversely affect the job that he did.

The end of the decade also saw the second woman elected to a statewide office in Mississippi. The majority of Mississippi voters supported Amy Tuck for lieutenant governor and I supported her through the Voters' League. We strongly endorsed her and as a result helped her win the election. Tuck was a Democrat, but after she was elected she changed to the Republican Party. In the state of Mississippi the law is written in such a way that it is fairly easy for elected officials to switch parties without any repercussions. The rule in some other states is that once a candidate wins under a declared party affiliation, the person can't switch parties until after the term is served. I feel the voters suffer an injustice when an elected official can switch parties like Tuck did. In my opinion when she switched parties it betrayed those who supported her in part because they also believed in and were loyal to the party she claimed to represent. Lieutenant Governor Tuck worked with the Democrats and she did, perhaps, as much as she could in this regard, considering her new Republican status. She reappointed me to the Municipalities Committee but she also appointed other African Americans who were Democrats to various positions, despite the fact that she had switched parties.

I believe the state of Mississippi in 2001 suffered one of the greatest defeats in its history. We did it to ourselves; hence we have no one but our own citizens to blame for it. In this year, there was a golden opportunity to change the image of the state by adopting a new state flag, but instead the issue turned into a divisive controversy and a tremendous disappointment for progress. The state held an allegiance to a flag that some viewed as symbolically tied to slavery and Jim Crow oppression. At the end of 2000 Governor Ronnie Musgrove formed a committee to change the Mississippi flag. Former governor William Winter was appointed to chair the committee. Winter was perhaps the most liberal governor in Mississippi history and he always pushed for progressive change. Prominent on the committee also were African American attorneys and state legislators. Governor Musgrove was strongly in favor of the bill to change the flag. I thought we had a good chance to make this forward move since both he and Governor Winter were Democrats. The flag had always been referred to as a rebel flag because of its historic relationship to southern Confederacy. The proposed new flag would be devoid of the Confederate-era crossbars. The Voters' League immediately endorsed the new flag because we wanted a more race-friendly symbol, something that would convey thoughts of unity rather than division. We believed Mississippi was ready for a change and a new flag would symbolize our growth as a state.

I actually thought it would be an easy referendum for the state to pass, but it turned into a heated controversy. The committee began holding open public meetings in various parts of the state. The committee spoke at Mississippi Delta Community College, which brought out a very hostile crowd. The African American senators from the Delta made sure we were present to support endorsing the new flag proposal. Senators Willie Simmons, Johnnie Wall, and I hoped to convince the crowd that changing the flag would change the image of the state of Mississippi. Many of us felt the old flag was simply a hindrance to the progress of the state.

Governor Winter opened up the meeting by discussing the major reasons for changing the flag. The crowd was quite resistant to what the governor had to say. When it was my turn to address the crowd, it appeared that the people became more disruptive. They waved large rebel flags in the air and started hollering the word *watermelon* repeatedly. I assumed that was in reference to the stereotype whites have popularized about African Americans loving to eat watermelons. I totally ignored the hostile crowd and continued with my presentation. I stated that for African Americans the flag was a constant reminder of the harsh slavery days. The crowd had already decided to close their minds to any possibilities of change. White opposition to the new flag was largely based on the view that the current flag was part of their heritage and they didn't want to abandon it. In the book *Mississippi Politics*, by Jere Nash and Andy Taggart, the authors claim that in the various statewide meetings held to address the issue, the crowd at the community college was the most disruptive one. The atmosphere was so charged that elected officials had to be escorted by the police as they walked through the corridors. The crowd became so angry that some of them had the audacity to get into Governor Winter's face and call him a disgrace to the state of Mississippi. Winter, always a mild-mannered man, did his best to ignore the ignorance displayed by so many of these people. It was very disappointing to me to see that some of the people who were being disruptive were citizens from my own county. I was also shocked to learn that there were even some black leaders who claimed they had no problem with the flag. I could understand that people had a right to their own opinions, but I found it difficult to maintain a level of respect for black leaders who did not or could not understand why the flag issue was racially offensive and a real barrier to Mississippi's progressive advancement.

In the statewide vote on the new flag issue, the provision failed miserably. There was a huge disparity in the vote and I was quite disappointed in our defeat. Mississippians voted 65 percent to 35 percent to keep the current flag. The voter turnout in the election was small, largely because the issue was on the ballot in a nonelection year. This might have also influenced the outcome, particularly the vast percentage difference by which new flag support lost. There was a lot of controversy and acrimony concerning the flag issue. Indeed, the continuing controversy influenced the reelection defeat that Governor Musgrove later suffered. In the midst of our disappointment, however, our eyes were opened to the harsh reality. We realized that things in Mississippi had not changed as much as we once thought they had. Defeat aside, I had to move past this battle to engage others.

It was during the period when the flag issue raged that Chris was in a major automobile accident. The accident was serious enough that it kept her hospitalized for two months in Jackson. She had suffered some serious injuries and her condition made for a very delicate time for me as well. She was the most important person in my life and whatever she suffered I, too, suffered. I was extremely grateful that God allowed my wife to heal and return to her family.

The next legislative bill to debate involved tort reform, which also became a big battle. A major provision of the proposed law prohibited an individual from suing a company for more than a million dollars. The lawsuits that were being filed came mainly from predominantly black counties where African Americans controlled the government. The trial lawyers of Mississippi were against the tort reform law because of its dollar limits and because it could also adversely affect the fees they earned. It became an even greater issue because trial lawyers often pushed for African American juries in the cases they litigated. There had been numerous cases where a company was sued for millions of dollars and the plaintiff was awarded a large settlement by a black jury. Tort reform also restricted jurisdiction in which the incident occurred. The bill required that out-of-state lawyers representing Mississippians in these kind of suits be admitted to the Mississippi bar prior to handling the case.

Many easily saw tort reform as another effort to discriminate against black people. It was almost as if white tort reform advocates did not trust black Mississippians to exercise any ability to reason or judiciously chart a course of what is right or wrong in a court of law. For many of these advocates the inference was that only white jurors were smart enough to make reasonable decisions in lawsuit cases. Moreover, by implication, they sought to restrict black redress for various kinds of wrongs through one of the most logical and fundamental kinds of remedies available to American citizens. There were cases where African Americans had been severely hurt at their place of employment or their health had been seriously damaged in some form as a result of corporate negligence. I strongly believe that if there is an injustice done to anyone, then the responsible party should be held accountable. We were in session concerning this bill from September until November, longer than our regular session, and we did everything in our power to keep it from becoming a law. Its opponents were unsuccessful in preventing it from becoming law. The bill passed after Thanksgiving, its major feature making one million dollars the statutory limit for a lawsuit.

At the end of 2002 the legislature put physical education back into Mississippi public schools. After desegregation began, somehow physical education got slowly phased out of the curriculum. It wasn't until child obesity became a recognized national problem that we decided that the time had come to address it in Mississippi by putting physical education back into the schools. Given the many health problems that ensue from obesity, I'm convinced that this was one of the greatest contributions that we could have made to public education in recent years.

On November 4, 2003, Governor Musgrove was defeated by Haley Barbour for the office of governor. Barbour received 53 percent of the votes to become the sixty-third governor of Mississippi and just the second Republican governor elected in the state since Reconstruction. He was determined to build on the tort reform law that had been passed during the Musgrove administration. In his initiative, Barbour focused on standards of medical care or malpractice suits. As was the case in earlier tort reform, monetary award limits were placed on plaintiffs who successfully won their injury suits against liable provider-defendants based on malpractice or breaches in standards of care. Because the bill as passed decreed a maximum award of only five hundred thousand dollars in these kinds of cases, many people have described it as the most restrictive in the nation.

In July of 2004 I traveled to Boston, Massachusetts, as a delegate to attend the Democratic National Convention. We nominated John Kerry and John Edwards for the presidency and vice presidency. I had previously met Kerry when he visited the state of Mississippi. The highlight of the convention was the keynote speaker, little-known Chicago community organizer Barack Obama. At the time he was an Illinois candidate for the United States Senate. I remember listening to him and thinking what a dynamic speech he was delivering. He spoke about the importance of unity and how Americans must perceive of themselves as one people. And he stressed the importance of hope in America, a theme he would also stress in a future run for the presidency. Obama went on to emphasize how the lives of Americans could be improved with the right governmental policies being in place. The crowd was completely moved by his speech and showed their enthusiasm and support for his thoughts by giving him a standing ovation as he made his way to his seat. There are many who believe that it was this keynote address that allowed Obama to win the Democratic presidential nomination in 2008. He spoke with so much confidence, but perhaps it was the vision and optimism about America that he articulated so well that earned him the presidential seat four years later. These were defining moments for me about Obama and they inspired me to stay upbeat and keep moving forward in my own life.

We had suffered two major recent defeats that appeared to mainly affect African Americans, but we couldn't hold our heads down and ponder over the losses. I felt the flag issue continued to leave an ugly mark on the state of Mississippi because of the racism that it seemed to represent. I truly believed that in order for us to put the past behind us a new flag would have been crucial. Moreover, in my opinion, the tort reform law also adversely affected African Americans because it possibly removed substantial financial gains from an equation that could have changed the lives of many families in the black community. I still believed that we had a lot of work ahead of us and I was committed to doing my part to make sure that we stayed focused. I knew that persevering to pass beneficial bills through the legislature would serve to upgrade living conditions in the state of Mississippi for all our citizens.

Mississippi Blues

The Mississippi Blues Bill suggested by the Blues Commission was certainly a bill that I was very proud to author. The purpose of the bill was to develop a plan to promote authentic Mississippi blues music for the purpose of economic development and to empower the African American culture that created it. To accomplish these goals, the bill sought to increase revenue from tourism, conferences, music performances, filmmaking, and other things through the promotion of the music genre and the heritage and culture that produced it. Few people were not visionary enough to see and understand the benefits the state could accrue from the bill, so fifty-two senators, a solid majority, voted to pass it. I felt it was only fair to implement a bill of this nature considering the history behind the blues. The music genre originated in African American communities primarily in the Deep South, notably the Mississippi Delta. I had invited B. B. King, a Mississippi Delta native and an icon of the genre, to Mississippi to be honored a year earlier. Certainly there was no greater person to represent the history of blues than the legendary B. B. King. In February of 2005 he came home to accept my offer.

We met him at the airport and escorted him right to the hotel where we had made accommodations for him. The next morning we picked him up and brought him to the capitol. The crowd had begun gathering in every level of the senate and I was later told that this was the biggest crowd ever drawn to the senate. Morgan Freeman had once been a guest at the capitol and even he didn't command a crowd of this magnitude. This was definitely a day for a King as he walked into the chambers. His famous song titled "The Thrill

Is Gone" reverberated through the monitors and the crowd went wild. It was simply amazing and I was quite proud to be a part of such a special celebration. Escorts guided him to his seat and I went through the preliminaries of requesting privileges of the floor for him. B. B. King finally made his way to the podium and all the African American senators and the other guests who wanted to be a part of this wonderful occasion gathered around him. There were medical personnel present because it was a known fact that King suffered from diabetes. We wanted to be extra cautious and provide as much comfort as possible while he was present. King had visited many capitols all over the world, but he had never been honored this way in his home state. A native of Indianola, Mississippi, he had finally returned home to be honored.

As tears streamed down his face, the legendary blues musician spoke about how he felt like the prodigal son. It was rather emotional for me to witness him being celebrated in the Mississippi state legislature. We spent a couple of hours listening to blues music as King took photos and shook hands with the Mississippi crowd. We left to go to our next destination, which was a luncheon at the Governor's Mansion where the great time continued. Later that night King performed at a club for those who were unable to attend the capitol event. There was also the Blues Musician Workshop at Mississippi Valley State University that King attended. It was a workshop set up to honor young aspiring musicians—to encourage them to keep pursuing their dream and to continue working on their craft.

Later in the year there was a groundbreaking ceremony for the B. B. King Museum. It took three years and fifteen million dollars before the B. B. King Museum opened up in his hometown. The museum is a great tourist attraction; it covers all aspects of his life, which includes his difficult childhood in the Mississippi Delta. This is a great honor for a great man who definitely deserves it. He returns to the museum at least once a year to show his gratitude. It is even more gratifying that B. B. King has lived long enough to see that the Mississippi Delta of his youth had made some major positive changes over the decades.

In Greenwood we were preparing to elect the first female and the first African American mayor. Democratic mayoral candidate Sheriel Perkins was preparing for the election against her opponent, Republican Mayor Harry Smith. The Voters' League was in full support of Mrs. Perkins because we knew that she would be a leader who would be dedicated to the welfare of the people. She was also a member of the city council and had a long-time association with the Voters' League. Mrs. Perkins visited the Voters' League to encourage the members to get as many voters to the polls as possible. She also thanked the Voters' League for doing everything possible to get her elected. African Americans in the city of Greenwood were hoping to witness history being made with a Perkins victory.

We were victorious in the election, or at least we thought we were. We were sure that Sheriel Perkins was now the mayor of Greenwood, but that wasn't the case. I learned when I came back from Jackson that a box of ballots had been found in north Greenwood. The margin that Mrs. Perkins had supposedly won by was over four hundred votes, but when this previously uncounted voting box surfaced it gave Harry Smith a six-vote victory margin. We couldn't believe it and we were forced to take the case to court. Mayor Harry Smith stayed in office for a year and a half while Representative Willie Perkins launched his own research on what actually occurred in the election.

Meanwhile in Chicago, old bones were being dug up. The U.S. Department of Justice decided to reopen the Emmett Till investigation. The body of Till was buried at the Burr Oak Cemetery in Alsip, Illinois, and it was exhumed by authorities there to begin the investigation. The investigators were hoping to determine the cause of death and to see if any other evidence could be found to help Mississippi officials bring additional charges, if warranted. There were many questions about why it took the federal government so long to reopen the case. If there was justice to eventually come from this hideous crime the only negative derived from it would be that Mamie Till wouldn't be around to witness it.

In the meantime, I was pushing another bill through the legislature. It dealt with the erection of a highway monument in remembrance of Emmett Till. The Emmett Till Memorial Highway Marker was erected in July of 2005. I had actually gotten the bill passed in May, but there were preliminaries that we had to go through first with the highway commission board. The sign dedicated a portion of U.S. 49 in honor of Till. It was a special tribute for a young boy who certainly left an everlasting mark in African American history. Meanwhile the body that was exhumed from Burr Oak Cemetery was legally identified as Emmett Till though there was never any doubt from the start in most people's minds that the body in the grave was actually that of the fourteen-year-old boy. The defense at the trial, however, had sought to establish doubt when it tried to advance suspicion that a body had been planted in the Tallahatchie River by the NAACP to stir up trouble and it wasn't the body of Emmett Till. Little else has occurred to bring finality to the investigation since this initial move to reopen the case, however.

In August of 2005 the southern United States was hit by Hurricane Katrina, causing the nation to suffer the most costly natural disaster in history. Besides New Orleans, the most serious damage occurred in coastal Mississippi, where some towns were flooded over 90 percent of their land mass. Of course, we didn't know it was as bad as it was until days later when we had adequate time to assess the damage all along the Gulf Coast. The state government was forced to call a special session to deal with the unexpected life-altering crises that thousands of Americans faced. Shortly after the storm made landfall, I traveled to Jackson, with weather conditions still a little unsettled. The senators were gathered in the senate and that is where I ran into many of them. Some of them had tears in their eyes as they grieved over the terrific damage that had occurred. The state needed millions of dollars to help provide the victims with some immediate relief and stability, but there was almost instant debate over the issue of necessary emergency funds. I don't know if the reason was because of the remnants of historic intrastate regional rivalries or simply because north and east Mississippi and the Delta were not adversely affected by Katrina, but clearly the Gulf Coast counties needed substantial help. One of the senators finally opened up the discussion, and his description of the problems was telling. There were people who had no place to live—thousands were literally left homeless and hopeless. The downtown commercial centers on the coast were devastated by the storm. There were cities that had been flooded, others completely blown away. The Treasure Island Casino, one of the gambling venues that provided considerable tax revenue to the state's coffers, had been lifted up by the water and carried across the interstate. It was quite clear that immediate revenue was needed for these hard-hit areas and the constant redundant debating about it began to cause dissention. I finally got an opportunity to approach the podium. I said, "We should be ashamed of ourselves. We have Mississippians who have suffered from a national disaster and we're taking time out debating on whether we should allow the victims the money that would provide them some type of relief until they can begin to repair." There were mostly white Republicans in the senate chambers listening to the logical points that were being made concerning this issue. A couple of senators spoke after I did and then we voted in favor of providing the relief. The bill then went to the house of representatives and there were debates as well, but logic prevailed and the senate bill passed. Although we didn't always vote together, I embraced my fellow colleagues because we still shared human compassion.

A month later I was asked to attend a press conference on the Gulf Coast. Chris accompanied me to Jackson and from there I took a bus to the coast while Chris stayed behind shopping. I was able to see the disaster areas with my very own eyes. I remember there was a small town called Waveland, Mississippi, and the only thing left there were the steps of city hall. There was debris at least twelve to thirteen feet high surrounding us. I was completely stunned by the pervasive damage that had occurred from the hurricane. I sat down on the steps in disbelief and wondered what was underneath all that debris. It was explained that the waves were forty feet high coming from the gulf. A wall of water that high was just as powerful as the wind. The community college was demolished as well as large areas on the air force base. The place was just an eyesore; everywhere one looked there was destruction. Injury and death were just as emotionally painful to realize. At some point during the cleanup there were corpses discovered almost everywhere; the death toll in the state of Mississippi eventually totaled over two hundred. The Mississippi Gulf Coast is sixty miles from New Orleans where there were more damages and more deaths. It was difficult not to be teary-eyed from all the human suffering the catastrophe caused.

There were many people out of work and during the rebuilding process the legislature obviously had to address this, too. Many of the jobless were those affected by the destruction of the casinos. Largely because of their water-based situation, confined in such a way by state law, this industry had frequently convulsed in the wake of similar gulf weather patterns. Not only did it affect the bottom line of businesses themselves, but also the flow of state revenue. The severe damages that the coastal casinos experienced this time, however, prompted the legislature during the rebuilding process to allow them later to move from their water moorings to permanent inland-based locations.

Obviously it was a very sad and traumatic time, with so many people being affected by this kind of destruction. The cost financially for Mississippi was clearly staggering, estimated at over one hundred billion dollars, but there could never be a dollar amount on the extent of human suffering, especially on the number of lives that were lost.

The Katrina tragedy occurred around the same time that I was up for reelection to the city council. I had two opponents, one of whom was George Ellis. Mr. Ellis decided that his campaign strategy was going to be passing out fish dinners. I guess someone must have advised him that passing out dinners would be a great way to gain votes. He made sure that on Friday and Saturday as many people from all over the district as he could reach had a plate. The election came and I was victorious by a very slim margin of votes against both candidates. Mr. Ellis and his team felt the election was too close, so they challenged the outcome. Their main argument was that some of the votes for me weren't legitimate. They called for another election and immediately filed a suit to do so. A judge from the Supreme Court was appointed to hear the case and the decision came down ordering another election, forcing me to defend a seat that I had already won!

To Defend until the End

I wasn't pleased with the fact that the judge was ordering another election. There had already been a recount and the outcome was the same—that I had beaten both opponents. I shouldn't have been too surprised about the court's decision, however, because I had often found myself in battles where I was forced to defend my position. The fact that the vote was so close made it a great possibility for many that I could have actually lost the election. There was also reason to discard a couple of ballots and that was all the ammunition my opponent needed to request another election. The judge set the reelection for January 10, 2006. I decided not to do any campaigning because I strongly felt that I had already been victorious in this battle. The first week of January is when the legislature session always begins. This was going to be only the second time that I missed the senate's opening in twenty years and as far as I was concerned the reason wasn't valid. I was going through a process that had already been determined, but I was confident that I would claim another victory. My opponent, George Ellis, began to campaign the same as he had done in the previous election. He still believed that fish dinners were ammunition for defeating me and he began passing out plates again. I received support from the senate and collected campaign contributions that totaled close to two thousand dollars.

A few days before the election a tour group visited the Leflore County Courthouse. I was asked to lecture to the group about the importance of the Emmett Till murder case and how it sparked the civil rights movement. The tour was organized by Dr. Bernard LaFayette, who was the director of the Center for Nonviolence and Peace Studies at the University of Rhode Island. The tour group included teachers and students from New Jersey, Georgia, Rhode Island, and Maryland. I had become accustomed to speaking to tourists and any chance that I got to educate people on African American history I considered to be quite rewarding. I also discussed the importance of placing a monument to Emmett Till on the courthouse grounds. I said, "Just as they display the Civil War stuff. . . . They have all of their heroes. Now it's only fair and fitting and proper that we have ours." The tourists listened closely to my lecture before boarding a bus headed to Money, Mississippi. I was more than privileged to address a crowd with such significant historical information.

On the night before the election I learned that the Election Commission wanted to place white individuals over my ward to assist in the election. I was totally against the whole idea and I immediately rejected it. I was more than willing to take full responsibility for what occurred in this election. The voters were quite aware of what this race was all about and everyone was anxious to learn the outcome. The morning of the election was cold and rainy. I went to the precinct and Representative Willie Perkins arrived to aid me. I stayed all day and made sure that the people who were assisting me had lunch. All the activities that transpired were being heavily monitored because it was obvious that Mr. Ellis was anxious for a victory. When the ballots were counted, I was victorious by over 71 percent of the votes. I believe the margin was greater this time because it was a one-on-one race instead of me running against two opponents. I was glad the election was over, and so were the individuals who wanted to see me back in office.

The year after the Emmett Till marker was erected it was defaced. It was a summer night in June of 2006 when this painful reminder showed that racism still existed in Mississippi. The letters "KKK" appeared boldly in bright-red paint on the sign. An inexcusable act of this nature immediately made many Mississippians think back to a case where justice had never been served. Some people believed that the vandalizing of the sign was triggered by the reopening of the Till case in 2005. The case was being reviewed to see if there were any charges that could be made against Carolyn Bryant. The woman who had ignited the brutal killing of Emmett Till was the only living suspect. The others, J. W. Milam and Roy Bryant, who had been tried and acquitted for the Till murder, were now deceased. A decision had still not been reached on what the district attorney was going to do with the investigation, but it appeared that someone was reminding us of the hatred attached to this case. I felt the vandalism was a stupid and cowardly act and I received phone calls about the incident from all over the nation. The local authorities began investigating and asked anyone with information to come forward. There were many who were now questioning if racism would ever truly be buried and if equality would ever exist. We were determined to replace the sign as soon as possible and were still committed to working with whites to bring real racial progress to Mississippi.

Willie Perkins's persistence in behalf of Sheriel Perkins's mayoral contest finally paid off for him. The judge ordered another election set for September. We strongly believed that Sheriel Perkins had already won the mayoral election back in 2005, but we were confident that she would be victorious again. When the results came back there was no doubt that Sheriel Perkins was the new mayor of Greenwood. She had won the election by almost three hundred votes and made history in the process. She was the first African American mayor for the city of Greenwood. The unfortunate part was that a year and a half had already passed out of her four-year term. I considered her victory to be a classic example of believing that what God has for you no man can stop. We would have been completely satisfied simply to see her serve the four-year term that she earned, but we showed that in a larger sense we were willing to defend positions based on what is right, no matter the sacrifice. We had a black mayor and we strongly believed that we could get some things accomplished with her in office. Mayor Perkins visited each district with her staff to find out the needs of the people. It gave the citizens an opportunity to express their complaints to the mayor and her administration. I thought it was a great idea because she had the personality and the right attitude to engage in personal interactions with the people. The techniques that Sheriel Perkins employed were definitely a great fit for the city of Greenwood and I felt that she was an excellent mayor.

In February of 2007, the Leflore County grand jury decided not to indict Carolyn Bryant. She had maintained her innocence from the beginning. The FBI had presented Leflore County District Attorney Joyce Chiles with an eight-thousand-page report on the Emmett Till case that identified Bryant as a suspect. The night that Till was carried away from his uncle's home, it was stated that a woman's voice, believed to be that of Carolyn Bryant, identified Emmett to the two men tried for his murder. I was terribly disappointed that there was no indictment in this second round. Mose Wright's cousin, Simeon Wright, was also quite surprised at the grand jury's decision because he was looking for an indictment. He stated that he would have loved to have been present while the jury deliberated and analyzed the evidence. Mr. Wright felt that the grand jury's decision only deprived Carolyn Bryant of an opportunity to absolve herself of any responsibility in Till's death. It was no secret that Roy Bryant and J. W. Milam died with Emmett Till's blood on their hands. The state of Mississippi would have to accept that justice really hadn't prevailed for such a heinous crime. We would not, however, let a bad decision made from higher officials keep us from honoring his memory. Mrs. Bryant would have to hear about this case for the remainder of her life because it was obvious that the world would never forget Emmett Till.

It was time for the primary election for the state senate. An independent opponent was running against me in the general election. My opponent was a man who had participated in some of the marches that I had led. It wasn't until after we began campaigning that I was suddenly disappearing in the pictures from these marches. The only part of my body identifiable in some of them was my feet. I found this laughable because everyone knew that I led the marches and had done so for quite some time. I was not overly concerned, however, because this was politics and doctoring the photos, along with his widespread use of political yard signs, were part of a strategy to defeat me in the upcoming election.

Right after the primary was over someone fired a bullet into my front door. I had had two visitors that day in my home to discuss the opening of the Emmett Till Museum. We sat around talking for a few hours bouncing ideas and opinions off of each other. It was a decent gathering and when they left I felt good about our discussion. I walked to the back of the house and checked on Chris, who was in another room relaxing. I returned to the den and immediately noticed that the glass was shattered on the storm door. I looked at the upper left corner of the door and saw a bullet hole. I called the police chief and asked if he would come to my home. When he arrived I opened the door and at that point, the whole glass fell out. He inspected the scene to see if he could possibly locate a bullet, but he didn't discover one. The case was turned over to the FBI, who came out and took pictures of the scene. I provided the investigation authorities, local and federal, with all the information that I had and left things in their hands. There were people who actually believed that I fabricated the whole story. I thought it was absolutely ridiculous for some to feel this way, but these were people who really didn't know David Jordan anyway. Besides, I knew how some people looked for any reason to make me out to be a villain. There was certainly nothing that I could possibly gain from destroying my own property. I had no idea what had triggered this cowardly incident and endangered my wife who has absolutely nothing to do with the political battles that I encountered, but given the broad-based nature of my activism the possible motivations were numerous. I never knew who was observing me or my residence and that was a very uncomfortable feeling. The people of Greenwood and Leflore County were certain of one thing, and that was that I wasn't afraid to confront issues of racism and injustice, and if this was the perpetrator's major incentive, I would still not be deterred. If my political actions were making someone this uneasy I would rather they acquire the courage to confront me directly. There was no need for anyone to be so disgruntled over anything that could easily be resolved when handled in the proper manner.

During this time I was getting considerable recognition for my political work. I received a plaque for my twenty years of service on the city council. The Mississippi Municipal League honored me and this gave me great pride. I had fought to serve in dual office and this was a recognition of my dedication to the positions that I held. I was still honoring people in the state senate. I made sure that I sought out every black man or woman who was a native Mississippian who was making a positive difference in our world. This time I invited Lerone Bennett to be honored; he was the executive director of *Ebony* magazine and a reputable historian of African American history. He was also an excellent writer, the author of several books, including *Before the Mayflower,* his most well-known study of black history. He made a dynamic speech and impressed the crowd that was gathered in the senate chambers to honor him. He was surprised to see how far the state of Mississippi had come in terms of African American elected officials. Bennett appeared to be very happy about the honor. I was quite pleased to be a part of the special meeting that we held with him.

The memory of Emmett Till constantly stirred up a lot of emotions that were good and bad. His name was a reminder that after all these years racism is still a reality. The Emmett Till Memorial Highway marker was once again in the news headlines. This time vandals chose not to smear degrading words across the sign, but to make it disappear totally. I was very disgusted when I learned that the sign was gone. I couldn't believe that someone had enough time to uproot the sign and not be noticed. It was also shocking to accept such a bold act. Meddling with the sign this way was a reminder of the mockery of justice that was involved in punishing those responsible for Till's death. The sign was significant to all of us and certainly for African Americans in the South. I wanted tourists to see how far the state of Mississippi had come by naming a highway after Emmett Till and for it to just disappear in the way it did was an outrage. This was a clear case of what I considered to be reopening of old wounds. However, the highway department did replace the Emmett Till sign within ten days.

In 2008, I introduced a resolution asking the state of Mississippi to officially apologize for the murder of Emmett Till. The measure was quickly defeated. Some colleagues based their opposition on the fact that they and most Mississippians had absolutely nothing to do with what happened to Till, hence no official state apology was necessary. Still, some apologetic sentiment was being unofficially expressed and this progress gave me added optimism that one day the state of Mississippi would do the right thing and show deep sympathy for what happened in the Till incident. At the time I thought back to the 1996 Democratic National Convention that was held in Chicago when Bill Clinton was nominated for reelection. There was a company there that sponsored the Mississippi breakfasts that allowed the state delegation to bond more closely. Former governors William Winter and Ray Mabus were present. Black attorney and senator Johnnie Walls was chairman of the Democratic Party. While in Chicago, Walls was determined to locate Mrs. Mamie Till and he was able to find her. Senator Walls went by her home and requested that she join the Mississippi delegation for breakfast. We were pleased that she accepted the offer and made an appearance.

Mrs. Mamie Till was then extended a very sincere apology from both governors for the brutal death of her son. She accepted their humble apology. To be sure, the gesture was a long time coming, but it was progress in the right direction. During the encounter Mrs. Till freely discussed her emotion about the tragic incident. According to Governor Winter in his conversation with her in 1996, she said, "There was one time I hated the name of Mississippi. I never wanted to hear the name of Mississippi, but after observing what is transpiring in Mississippi, I wouldn't mind relocating." We all knew that an apology couldn't erase the pain and suffering that Emmett Till and his family endured, but I hoped this was the beginning in a real healing process between Mississippi and the Till family!

Apology Accepted

In October of 2007 I was the master of ceremonies for a very remarkable event in Tallahatchie County. The event was held for the purpose of formally apologizing to the Till family for the injustice that occurred in 1955. There were people from all over the country in attendance for this monumental celebration, including some of Till's relatives from Chicago. The only regret regarding the occasion was that Mamie Till had died in 2003 without seeing justice for her son, though she had graciously accepted the heartfelt apologies of two former Mississippi governors several years prior to her death. I was thrilled that the ceremony was being held at the Tallahatchie County Courthouse in Sumner. It was the same place where a not-guilty verdict for the accused murderers caused an uproar in African American communities all over the country. There were approximately four hundred people in attendance to witness this formal program. Many respected dignitaries approached the podium and made very significant remarks. Available for viewing was a printed resolution bearing the names of a number of elected officials who knew the black mark this injustice had left on the state of Mississippi. I read resolutions from state representatives Tommy Reynolds of Charleston and Robert Huddleston of Sumner who were unable to attend. I also read a personal resolution for Congressman Bennie Thompson of the second congressional district. My own personal remarks were simply this: "Those who committed this heinous crime meant for it to be evil, but God is a just God. He brought positive results from it. It changed the mood of the country and gave African Americans the right to vote and hold public office." After the program ended a historical marker from the Mississippi

Department of Archives and History was unveiled by Jerome Little. The president of the board of supervisors presented the honor. The text of the Emmett Till Memorial Commission's Resolution read as follows:

We the citizens of Tallahatchie County believe that racial reconciliation begins with telling the truth. We call on the state of Mississippi, all of its citizens in every county, to begin an honest investigation into our history. While it will be painful, it is necessary to nurture reconciliation and to ensure justice for all. By recognizing the potential for division and violence in our own towns, we pledge to each other, black and white, to move forward together in healing the wounds of the past, and in ensuring equal justice for all of our citizens. Over fifty-one years ago, on August 28, 1955, fourteen-year-old Emmett Till was kidnapped in the middle of the night from his uncle's home near Money, Miss., by at least two men, one from Leflore and one from Tallahatchie County, Miss. Emmett Till, a black youth from Chicago visiting family in Mississippi, was murdered, and his body thrown into the Tallahatchie River. He had been accused of whistling at a white woman in Money. His badly beaten body was found days later in Tallahatchie County, Miss. The grand jury meeting in Sumner, Miss., indicted Roy Bryant and J. W. Milam for the crime of murder. These two men were then tried on this charge and were acquitted by an all-white all-male jury after a deliberation of just over an hour. Within three months of their acquittal, the two men confessed to the murder. Before the trial began, Till's mother had sought assistance from federal officials, under the terms of the so-called Lindbergh Law, which made kidnapping a federal crime, but received no aid. Only a renewed request in December of 2002 from Till's mother, supported by Mississippi District Attorney Joyce Chiles and the Emmett Till Justice Campaign, yielded a new investigation.

We the citizens of Tallahatchie County recognize that the

Emmett Till case was a terrible miscarriage of justice. We state candidly and with deep regret the failure to effectively pursue justice. We wish to say to the family of Emmett Till that we are profoundly sorry for what was done in this community to your loved one. We the citizens of Tallahatchie County acknowledge the horrific nature of this crime. Its legacy has haunted our community. We need to understand the system that encouraged these events and others like them to occur so that we can ensure that it never happens again. Working together, we have the power to fulfill the promise of liberty and justice for all!

The family of Emmett Till was quite appreciative of the remorse shown at the public ceremony and graciously accepted the apology. There was a special luncheon that immediately followed the program at R. H. Bearden Elementary School. I believe that Till's cousin, Wheeler Parker, of Summit Argo, Illinois, said it best when he stated, "Emmett speaks louder in death than he ever would have if he had lived!"

At the end of 2007 I was devoting myself to routine business in the senate and on the Greenwood City Council. We were still debating bills and moving toward accomplishing as many goals as possible. The economy was starting to take a slight dive and that was troubling to national and state leaders. Oil prices soared up and the real estate market began to fall. All of these negatives affected both the well off as well the working class everywhere. In my own personal domestic life Chris and I were getting along lovingly; she was enjoying spending quality time with the grandchildren, so her life was filled with meaningful activities. The children flourished in their employment, their education having served them well. Donald was in Texas working with Walmart as a pharmacist. Darryl was still working as a doctor in Nashville. Joyce was in Austin, Texas, working in the mayor's office, and David was still residing in California. They all were happy with their lives, and for this I was extremely grateful.

As the year 2008 began there was still a lot of debate concerning the proposed voter ID bill being passed. The legislature had unsuccessfully tried to get this bill passed for the past decade. I am totally against voter ID because in my opinion it's too similar to the hated poll tax. Before it was finally outlawed in the 1960s, the poll tax was used as a scheme in the South to keep the poor from voting by charging money to vote and in most instances this largely affected black people. Simply put, I feel that there are ulterior motives attached to those wanting this voter ID bill passed. In the state of Mississippi there has never been a single voting case where misidentification was the issue. It is also a known fact that the majority of the voters in Mississippi are senior citizens. They vote early and more consistently than anyone else, but seniors are also a group of people who would likely not have a driver's license, the most acceptable form of required voter ID. Hence, this is a bill that could possibly interfere dramatically with the number of voters that turns out on election day. It also slows up the electoral process because voters having to produce the ID could prompt long waiting lines at the precincts. Voter ID can also be an intimidating factor that could possibly deter voters from voting, especially black seniors who once faced various forms of threats for attempting to vote.

I could possibly have been persuaded to look at this in another light if I had ever heard of voter fraud, but I haven't. Supporters of the bill argue that such a law would maintain the integrity of elections in Mississippi, but it's just hard for me to believe that anyone would undertake any fraudulent effort of pretending to be someone else just to cast a vote. The bill usually gets passed in the senate, but fails in the house of representatives; it is back on the table for the upcoming November 2012 election. I have voted and spoken against it several times and will continue to do so if necessary. I still strongly believe that no bill should be passed that could perhaps have an adverse effect on the American voter. This is my personal feeling about the devilish voter ID: I remember an old man selling puppies one day at one dollar each. The next day he had those same puppies at two dollars each. Someone asked him why the price difference, and he said, "Their eyes are open." Our eyes are wide open and we know the trick; we know why this bill is being pushed here so determinedly by supporters and why we are spending valuable time dealing with it! We need to continue finding ways to encourage more people to vote instead of perhaps deterring them from voting.

Locally in Greenwood, there was another very important issue being debated and that was the closing of the Greenwood post office. The city of Greenwood was looking to purchase the Federal Building, site of the downtown post office, and put it up for sale to anyone who wanted to purchase it. I was very concerned about losing the post office because many elderly residents had learned to depend on it over the years. I felt that it would be the biggest handicap that the city would suffer because of the downtown Greenwood development. I was determined at all cost to fight for the post office to remain open, even if it meant I had another serious battle on my hands. I immediately began circulating a petition and I got more signatures than I had ever gotten in the past on other petitions. Despite the petition campaign, the post office was still sold. I was able to find out who purchased it, however. The mayor and I were able to meet with the owner, a man from California. I explained to him the position that the city of Greenwood would be in if the post office closed. He assured us that he would inform the city of Greenwood if he needed to occupy the space for his own purposes. He was definitely a man of his word because he did just that and allowed the post office to continue to function at the same location.

The forward steps that we make are only halted when we become negligent, making it easier to be pushed backwards. I believe that in this day and age we must place ourselves in positions that are instrumental to our growth as a people. I made a decision a long time ago that I would fight any issues where even an undertone of racism worked to undermine our racial progress. Many African Americans have paid extraordinary dues in the quest for black equality. Thus for us, the living, to readily accept the harsh words and brutal physical violence often perpetrated against us kicks dust on the graves of those brave heroes and heroines who paid the ultimate price in the struggle. I had come a long way from working on a plantation and I refuse to take lightly any form of disrespect based on my skin color. There are many who are quick to close their eyes to racism, but will judge their own people very harshly. I never quite understood that standard of thinking, considering that every step towards equality has come with a fight. I can't just sit back and allow any dastardly act against me and my people to occur without questioning the motives attached to them and then not working to bring the evildoers to justice. I know my views and opinions will not be accepted by everyone and I truly understand that, but I believe my thinking to be right and just. I don't understand, however, why my opinions provoke others into deceitful acts of vandalism or cowardly verbal attacks. I found myself in a position where I was forced to accept an apology for an act that I felt was unnecessary and quite degrading. The incident turned out to be confirmation that behind many supposedly kind eyes were still hidden traces of racism.

Not the N***** Word

It was March of 2008 and the legislative session was in progress, which meant I was spending the majority of my time in Jackson. I would drive to Greenwood for the city council meeting on Tuesday and that was my routine. Our council meetings could get quite intense and often councilmen would still be in discussion well after the meeting was adjourned. This one particular time Councilman John Lee and I left the meeting and stood around outside conversing about a few issues. There was an African American male in his late twenties across the street observing us. He finally hollered, "Hey, Senator Jordan." He immediately gained our attention and I recognized him as being a young man who had worked for me in one of the elections. He walked across the street and inquired if I had any employment available. It wasn't an election period, so at that time I had no work for him. John Lee stood silently observing our interaction and never once interrupted. The young man understood so we shook hands and he went on his way. I then focused my attention back on John and we continued our discussion. We eventually said our good nights and I left with the understanding that two city councilmen were just shooting the breeze after a meeting. This was customary, definitely not out of the ordinary. I had absolutely no reason to think a friendly conversation would turn into a major dispute.

A week passed. Chris and I drove up in the driveway and simultaneously a car was pulling up across the street. John Lee exited his vehicle and came rushing toward us. He handed me a letter and immediately began apologizing, but I had no idea what it was about. We all walked inside the house and I told John to have a seat in the den. I read the letter in complete silence, but I was disturbed over its content. John was in my home to soften the blow before I read his shocking remarks in the newspaper. The wrong source had obviously gotten hold of an e-mail intended for fifteen white people, one being a city councilman. I told John that he needed to leave and I would consider accepting his apology.

In the e-mail, John alleged that he had had a long talk after the city council meeting with David Jordan. "The ole nigger can't understand why the blacks continue to shoot one another. I told him he needed to spend less time with the old people at the Voters' League and more time with the young people about getting an education." John Lee's e-mail went on to claim that I missed my chance to help a "big black" who asked me for employment. I was stunned because the whole story had been fabricated and had no factual foundation. I was even more outraged that John felt that in this day and time I would quietly accept being called a "nigger" without any backlash. I was disturbed because this seemed to be routine behavior; John apparently felt quite comfortable sending this insulting e-mail to our colleagues. The e-mail issue made the headlines of the *Greenwood Commonwealth* and it disgruntled the vast majority of Greenwood's African American population. Many of them expressed disbelief that a highly respected black political leader was being referred to in this derogatory manner. There were a number of white people who were also angry with John and sent e-mails to the city's newspapers to express their disgust over his choice of words. It wasn't long before the news concerning the e-mail began to attract statewide and national media attention. It raised concerns that revamping the South may have been a distant dream and perhaps even a myth. There were African Americans all the way from Louisiana who wanted to organize a protest march, but I decided against it. *The Tom Joyner Morning Show* picked up the story and it also flooded the Internet.

I held a press conference at city hall to discuss the ugly situation. I expressed how shocked I was over the incident and said I had no idea why John would do something like this. I actually believed that we had a mutual respect for one another, but I was obviously wrong. Still, I didn't understand what he hoped to gain from the unflattering remarks. African Americans throughout the city wanted a public apology from John at our next council meeting. I was in full support of a public apology because it was obvious that his opinion concerning me was no longer a private issue.

The council meeting was filled with African American supporters. They wanted to know why John Lee hated black people and they also questioned the political position that he held. John became quite emotional from the pressure that he was receiving. I believe if there was ever anything that he wanted to take back it was those comments he made in reference to me in the e-mail. The tears began to well up in John Lee's eyes as he extended an apology to the city council, the community, the state, Chris, and to me. I accepted his apology, but I felt that John had damaged the image of Greenwood. I thought we would be able to work together at every level possible, but that was before I consulted with other members of the council for their views. I believed that for the continued growth of the city of Greenwood and for the African American race the best thing John Lee could do was to resign from his position and I said so.

The request for John Lee's resignation certainly stirred a lot of mixed reactions. I discovered the real views of a lot of my colleagues; I didn't receive the support from them that I believed I was entitled to. I know that words can't be taken back once they are expressed, but I believed there had to be some accountability beyond an apology. I just didn't believe that a man who had no respect for another man's differences could do the council any justice. I didn't believe he could fairly serve in a capacity where the majority of the population was African Americans. The first person to come to the aid of John Lee was another white councilman, Johnny Jennings. He felt that John Lee shouldn't resign because he had done a phenomenal job on the council. Jennings's actual comment stated, "You can listen to car stereos at McDonald's and hear worldwide role-model rappers using the 'n' word. Am I supposed to laugh? What am I supposed to do?

There are rappers that use it every third word. No matter what we do, everybody defaults to the 'Old South' and says, 'It is Mississippi, what do you expect?'"

I guess that statement was a means of justifying the blatant disrespect that I had suffered from another council member. There was no excuse for what had occurred. Though many people felt that I should just forgive and forget, doing so was difficult because this ordeal was quite painful to me. Jennings claimed that we should not be about destroying people for making mistakes. He said that if we can't forgive a man for mistakes of this kind, then the races in Mississippi would never make any progress. However, I didn't feel a mere apology that might not have been given sincerely anyway was sufficient. To me, something more punitive was warranted. For a public official to make purely racial remarks in Lee's language, severe consequences were in proper order. The other councilmen felt since there was no law, policy, or vote that could force John Lee to step down, then we were powerless to force him off the council. African American councilman Charles McCoy stated that the decision for Lee to step down was only Lee's decision to make. However, he felt that apologizing only to the other councilmen was not satisfactory and he supported the whole city of Greenwood receiving an open apology. Moreover, McCoy believed that a Lee resignation would allow the city to move forward in recruiting new employers. Councilman Tennill Cannon's position on the issue was that e-mail makes it difficult for us to function as a government. He disputed Jennings's claim of a double standard with the use of the n***** word. He stated that public officials, unlike rappers, are held to a higher standard of conduct, which should preclude using racist remarks because we are elected to be leaders. I couldn't have agreed more with Cannon's statement and that is why I felt it would have been in the best interest of the people for Lee to resign.

In an interview with Black America Web, state representative Willie Perkins expressed sentiments shared by many progressive-minded Mississippians. Perkins said, "John Lee's statement and presence do not help this community to move forward, which is what we need to do and move past John Lee and the many others here who are like him, but who have not expressed it. We've got to move past that group and continue to work with people of different colors to improve race relations, attract employment, and spur economic development." I finally had to come to the painful realization that this was a battle that I didn't have full support for. It was extremely disappointing the way things transpired because I would have stood with any of my African American colleagues if an injustice had occurred involving them. I thought it was ridiculous for John Lee to feel he was in a position to lecture me over what was best for any of my people. At best he certainly came out looking silly and uninformed. In extremely loud volume my track record had spoken for itself. I had sued just about everybody and every agency necessary in order for black Mississippians to have a measure of justice and opportunity. I had led demonstrations, reorganized the Voters' League, and led it for over forty years, and here someone like John Lee had the audacity to question how I could help one of my own. It was ridiculous and it was even more painful that some of my own people didn't see this as a disgrace. John Lee didn't resign, but it definitely placed a wedge between us and he was defeated the next time that he ran for office. I think the scandal that his racist words brought to the city of Greenwood contributed greatly to his defeat.

For me, it was back to routine business and as always I was forced to move past another unfortunate incident. There was more work to be accomplished and we could no longer cry over spilled milk. I was extremely grateful that the decision for the post office to remain open appeared to be solid for the next couple of years. The citizens of Greenwood were overjoyed because they strongly depended on the services and it was in a perfect location. The next major issue on the table was a health care facility opening in Leflore County.

The Mallory Health Center is a cluster of centers run by a group of African American entrepreneurs in Holmes County. A woman by the name of Dr. Martha Davis organized the first clinic in 1993 and named it after Mrs. Arenia C. Mallory, African American leader in education, religion, social welfare, and civil rights. I attended the groundbreaking ceremony for the first clinic. They went on to establish a total of three clinics in Holmes County, Madison County, and Carroll County. After Mrs. Davis passed away her daughter took over and continued to maintain the clinics. I had a road named in Mallory's and Davis's honor in Lexington, the Mallory-Davis Memorial Highway. They had done an excellent job in providing services for the underprivileged and I knew Mrs. Davis quite well. The centers wanted to expand into Leflore County and during that time Leflore County contacts actively worked to this end. I supported the Mallory Health Center coming to Leflore County because I thought it would be a beneficial service to the people. My motives were forthright—the service was legitimate and successful.

The Right Way
... Is My Way!

T hough I was in full support of the Mallory Health Center coming to Leflore County, unfortunately everyone didn't share my views. The controversy occurred because the federal government had not yet provided the resources for the county to establish a health clinic. The Mallory Health Center had the revenue at the time and they were already established. There were many citizens who wanted Mallory to come to Greenwood because they had a proven record of being excellent caregivers. They provided medical services for low-income people and charged them according to their income. The fee was prorated in such a way that anyone who needed health care was able to receive it. A local group of providers wanted to keep them away, but I saw no reason why they couldn't and shouldn't be in Leflore County. We needed services of their nature because they were beneficial to the underprivileged. I was the senator from Holmes and Leflore counties and I understood my constituents' needs; therefore, I was strongly in favor of the Mallory clinic serving Greenwood.

I invited the group that was in charge of the Mallory Health Center to the Voters' League meeting. I wanted to give them an opportunity to explain how instrumental it would be for them to provide services in Greenwood. The people supported the idea and wrote letters to that effect. I submitted two letters in support of Mallory, one as a state senator and one as president of the Greenwood Voters' League.

A Leflore County supervisor, Robert Collins, expressed dismay about my position, alleging that I supported the medical center without having conducted prior research on the issue. I didn't understand his comment because I attended the clinic's first groundbreaking ceremony. I had watched this clinic expand and I truly believed that people deserved a creditable place to visit for their health care. Mr. Collins felt that I had orchestrated the decision to ask for Mallory Health Center, but I was truly following the will of the people. It bothered Robert Collins because he was in charge of an effort to bring the county an alternative health center, one that would be run by white physicians. I didn't realize that he took the affair so personally until I read his comments in the *Greenwood Commonwealth*. Mr. Collins stated, "Senator Jordan has been a champion in the past, so people have said, so I've been told that he's been a champion for doing things for black people, but lately things that I see is that every time we get something started for Greenwood, some kind of way it gets bogged down back over in the Voters' League, or Senator David Jordan has something to do with it." In his opinion, the Voters' League was not capable of making a decision for everyone in the county. He added, "When you go down into the devil's den, it's either Senator Jordan's way or no way at all!"

There are individuals such as Robert Collins who have accused me of having my way, but that's absolutely not the case. The reality is that some of the issues that bring us together require debating. When I'm successful in making a better argument on a particular subject, then the losers find ways to salve their loss by accusing me of having my way. I find these types of accusations to be ludicrous because I don't even seek to get my way in my own household. How could a clinic being established in Greenwood for the underprivileged not be a good decision? The people should not have to suffer because Leflore County wasn't able to get the services as quickly as Mallory could. My objective has always been to see African Americans who run businesses expand as much as possible and to be in positions to serve their own people. Robert Collins is just one of many people who want to say David Jordan is trying to run everything. I put a slogan on my campaign literature that reads, "A Senator for the People." I try to live up to that statement by making life better for others. I try to meet the needs of the people in every situation that I deal with and I've been successful in achieving that goal. The Mallory Health Center is just one of many achievements I've been a part of over the years. I have found myself in the lion's den many times, but I state my position, follow up on what needs to happen, and just get it done. There are people who don't understand that and in my opinion it's simply because it's too much credit for an African American to receive. The Health Center would be beneficial to the black race and I and the Mallory people are black, plain and simple; therefore, I didn't understand the need for debate. I don't have time to always respond to preposterous allegations. Instead I try and get things accomplished and just move on. If people want to be upset and still foolishly debate over certain issues that is their prerogative. There is too much to be done to waddle in despair and bicker irrationally with uninformed people. I don't have time to address individuals who don't appear to have a positive and practical agenda.

It was a fall evening, November 5, 2008, a perfect day in my thinking to recognize a historic moment. I had just ended my long evening at the courthouse and I was headed home. I was handling the reelection campaign of Congressman Bennie Thompson and during this time I was keeping late hours. But something bigger than my work for Thompson was unfolding. It was around 8:00 p.m. on election day and I had been keeping up with the updates concerning the election. When I got home Chris was watching the election results in the bedroom. I walked in and quickly noticed that she was in tears. I immediately asked what was wrong. She said, "Dave, he just carried Florida." We were beginning to get excited, barely able to contain our emotions. The next state returns confirmed that Barack Obama had claimed the presidency. Chris and I celebrated like we were a group of ten people from the noise that we were making. We went through the house rejoicing over all the excitement. We celebrated until we saw an African American man and his family walk hand in hand and take center stage. I had never witnessed something so significant and gratifying in my life's journey for justice. My thoughts immediately turned to my daddy. He always spoke about one of his sons having an opportunity to meet the president of the United States. Not only had a black man become the president, but my daddy's son had had the opportunity to cast the Mississippi votes for him in the nomination convention. I was overwhelmed with history as I reminisced over my life. It was an exciting night filled with jubilation and one almost didn't know how to act. He received over sixty-six million votes, which meant other races joined in and helped Obama claim the presidential seat. It was such a glorious moment that we couldn't sleep.

As I was growing up, my daddy discussed with us the story about the rejected stone becoming the cornerstone of the building. This was in reference to Jesus Christ being rejected and yet becoming the foundation of hope for man and a world-renowned religion. The African American race has been rejected in many instances and now one of us had become the cornerstone of the United States. I didn't care what anyone might say that's negative about it because something truly great had happened. We elected a young African American president that every generation, from every race, could rejoice about. I never dreamed it would happen in my lifetime, but it became a reality.

I supported Obama from the very beginning. I was impressed with him when he gave his speech in Boston at the Democratic National Convention. I had never before heard of him and I had no idea where he had come from. I knew this man had made a lasting impression and I spoke highly of him with other members in the Mississippi Senate. When the Democratic nomination process for the presidential election began, everyone was geared up to support Hillary Clinton. I quickly told my fellow colleagues that there was another candidate that I might support. It was a couple of days later that attorney Brad Pigott came to my office and asked if I would sign on as a supporter for Barack Obama for president of the United States. I didn't hesitate to say yes. He gave me more information to sign up my fellow African American senators, but no one else would sign on with me. They believed that Hillary Clinton would win the nomination and she was definitely a strong competitor. I remember when she visited the state of Mississippi in March of the election year. I went to see her and I got an opportunity to shake her hand. I don't know if she remembered me, but she had come to the Voters' League with Congressman Mike Espy years before. Mrs. Clinton made a dynamic speech and the whole crowd responded quite well to her.

The next week I was invited by Congressman Thompson to accompany him in meeting Barack Obama. We met at Jackson State University and I brought my son Darryl along with me. We had made plans to spend the night in Jackson, and we were quite excited about meeting the future president. There were thirty-nine of us who were allowed to enter the meeting, but unfortunately Darryl wasn't able to get in. He didn't have the proper identification and he was disappointed at having to miss this golden opportunity. I shook hands with candidate Barack Obama and we took a couple of photos together. I had never met anyone before so full of life and he was obviously very intelligent. He appeared to be an easygoing person with a warm smile and very serious about making a difference. It was certainly a pleasure for me and I was elated to cast the Mississippi vote for him at the Democratic convention. I had supported an individual who many didn't believe stood a chance of winning.

The prospect of a black man running the country was something people had a hard time imagining. If there was one time that I had wanted my way it was seeing Barack Obama become president. I couldn't imagine a better way to end the year. Obama's victory had showed that it was time for African Americans to approach challenges with more confidence and less fear. We had made huge steps in our quest for equality and I felt that there was no goal unattainable. It didn't mean that by having an African American man running the country conditions would automatically become easy for blacks. We still had our work cut out for us, but President Obama had proved that anything is possible when we unite. I was more encouraged than ever now to move forward in continuing to make progress in African American lives.

In January of 2009 President Barack Obama was sworn in as the forty-fourth president of the United States of America. He had inherited a struggling economy that was sinking into a terrible recession, so he definitely had a lot of challenges ahead. In the beginning of this new era in the nation's life I was optimistically preparing for the upcoming city council election. My opponent, Larry Neal, who ran unsuccessfully against me for the senate seat, lived in the district and decided to challenge me for the city council position. As I prepared for the upcoming election, Greenwood received a visit from civil rights icon James Meredith, who came to the Delta to promote the importance of early childhood education and to observe the plight of the poor. Meredith, who had been the first to desegregate the University of Mississippi in 1962, was on a "Walk for the Poor" through the Delta counties, his journey being filmed for a documentary. I got an opportunity to speak with him at city hall. Meredith spoke about the value of teaching children their alphabets and numbers by the time they reach age five. He compared his journey to his famous "March Against Fear" from Memphis to Jackson to promote voting rights in 1966. Meredith was shot during his 1966 walk, but other leaders, including Dr. Martin Luther King Jr. and Dick Gregory, completed it.

I was very impressed with how Mr. Meredith addressed the city council. He stated that when the 1965 Voting Rights Act was passed and the Greenwood Voters' League was formed, the only thought was getting blacks the right to vote, not to have them govern. Meredith said, "The point is that we are no longer just voting. We are now ruling, but we're still blaming other people for the things that don't go right, and it's time for us to start ruling or give it up." He went on to talk about another purpose for his walk, which was to see the reality of what life had become in poor rural Delta towns where drug traffic and joblessness had taken a toll on the common man. I, along with councilmen Charles McCoy and Ronnie Stevenson, got an opportunity to walk with James Meredith in the downtown and Broad Street area. It was a valuable lesson from this iconic black civil rights activist. It probably was even more gratifying for Charles Mc-Coy, who was meeting James Meredith for the first time.

I thought about James Meredith's comments about blaming other people for the things that don't go right in our lives. I could definitely relate to this view because in my political activism I often bore the blame when the outcome of events or issues took a different turn than expected. I always approached every situation with the intent of effectively resolving a problem or controversy. The issues that turn into battles sometimes become necessary in order to meet and satisfy the needs of the people. I've always believed that when one's intent is pure things tend to work out favorably. I was approaching a time in my political career when people believed that ruling with an iron fist was no longer necessary. There was nothing wrong with change, but that didn't mean that leaders should ever compromise their positions. Those who are placed in leadership roles have been chosen to take on a greater responsibility, far beyond just the norm. I have been accused of being too pro-black. I am offended by those allegations because my responsibility is to the welfare of the people and to be fair in all of my efforts to insure their welfare. I speak the truth and when I think something needs to be corrected then I refuse to be silent about it. I reiterate that my helping African Americans acquire positions for which they are qualified has nothing to do with any alleged malice I have for the white race. I was chosen to be a voice for my people and there are certain issues that I would fight doggedly for or against to make sure that African Americans don't suffer any unfair treatment.

Not until Hell Freezes Over

In the city council election in the early fall of 2009, I defeated my opponent, Larry Neal, in the Democratic primary, winning nearly 65 percent of the vote. I then had an independent candidate run against me in the general election and I was victorious by approximately 70 percent of the votes to maintain my seat on the council. After we were sworn in and the new city council was in place, councilmen elected the president and secretary. I was the city council president and I was ready to yield my seat to the vice president, Mr. Ronnie Stevenson. The white citizens decided that they no longer wanted me to serve as president of the city council. It had been informed that by any means necessary I was to be prevented from maintaining that position. The white councilmen didn't really have the votes to oust me because there were five African Americans on the board, but I voluntarily agreed to step down at the end of the term. The African American councilmen also wanted someone new in the position, so I had no problem yielding my seat. I had been president a couple of times during my twenty-seven-year stint on the city council mainly because of the request of the community. Moreover, I was chairman of a committee in the senate. I had maintained an obligation over the years with the city and the state and was in a leadership capacity in both bodies, so it was imperative that I attend each meeting. Now, I no longer had that pressure and responsibility, although the city council voted me vice president. According to all accounts, the white community was elated to hear of my decision to step down as president. I had been accused of being "a hard nose," but I felt that I had been in the position long enough to know what are proper procedures as they relate to city and state government. I have twenty-seven years in city government and eighteen years in state government. When a person has been in office as long as I have, he discovers that many issues seem to repeat themselves. I was not worried about maintaining prestige as president. I was more concerned about the wheels of justice being lubricated to roll in the right direction for the people. I was very surprised that fellow African Americans found me to be too direct. In my observation I've learned that African Americans are a lot different in the hills of Tallahatchie County from those who reside in the Delta. Most black hill people may not have much, but they own their own land. Perhaps because of this their perception and ideas about life appear to be different from those of the sons and daughters of sharecroppers. There are still some African Americans who don't feel something is right unless "master" says it's right. Although I'm from the Delta and the son of a sharecropper, I certainly don't think along these lines. I learned early, based on the circumstances of my life, that I was going to be my own man. I thank the good Lord for blessing me with the opportunity to make this become a reality. I have worked extremely hard to overcome the many life obstacles that I've encountered. I don't have to grin unless I want to and I don't have to scratch unless I itch. I still see in a lot of young people who hold high positions the mentality of uncertainty and the need to compromise because they fear white displeasure will jeopardize their status. I don't understand why they feel and act the way they do and because I don't think and act like them, in many instances my difference is considered to be that of a malcontent or radical. I don't think God made a mistake because he made me black and the man I have turned out to be.

I delivered a speech on the day that I stepped down as council president. I made sure it was understood that I would support the new president. I would cooperate with him in every way possible because I was the oldest councilman and had the most experience. I thanked the city council and expressed how I had enjoyed the opportunity of serving as their president. We had a rather new city council of young African Americans on board. I wanted them to understand that we must continue to move forward because I didn't want all the previous accomplishments to be given back in short order. I had sued the city to change the form of city government and I was the first African American elected to the council. I worked extremely hard in order for African Americans to have some voice in city government. I look back over that journey and feel extremely good about it. There was no way that I wanted to see blacks lose what had been gained. It is when I see slippage that I'm forced to speak out about it. There are many who view that as being hard-nosed or too pro-black, but those are the ones who perhaps need a refresher course in African American history. We can't afford to compromise the positions that we have worked extremely hard to gain. We can't allow a white face to intimidate us because we feel inferior. It didn't matter what position I held during a battle when I thought our interests were not being handled correctly. It would take hell to freeze over before I stopped fighting for equality. Black people must continue to stand on our strengths and abilities and fight to maintain our rights.

It was right after the election that Governor Haley Barbour issued a proposal to merge Mississippi Valley State University with two other black universities. The governor wanted Valley State and Alcorn State University merged into Jackson State University. I was totally against it because Valley State was the only predominantly black four-year university in the Delta. I realized the economy was suffering, but Valley State University was too important to the region to risk doing anything that would harm its independent status. I was appalled anyway that Governor Barbour would recommend any sort of consolidation that involved closing or merging Valley. I wasn't the only one who objected to this proposal, so the rallies in support of Valley began. Each time that I went to Jackson for senate duty, there was someone rallying. I began speaking out against the merger because I was solidly opposed to it. I was the only senator who was a graduate of Valley State University, but I wasn't the only legislator; there were several graduates of Valley in the house of representatives.

I began campaigning in the Delta against the merger and I went to Greenville and made speeches. I spoke about it in the Voters' League meeting and in the churches. I held a hearing at the meeting hall in Greenville. I spoke anywhere that I could get an audience because I believed in Valley State University and in education as the only opportunity for black people's advancement. When I spoke in Jackson I addressed our history. I said, "We have given 247 years of free labor, 104 years of the worst type of discrimination, and now you're talking about merging our schools. You're talking about putting us under one roof—not until hell freezes over!" I went on to say that the only thing that the state college board would be closing is their mouths concerning this particular subject. It was right before the legislative session started that I went back to Greenville and made a big speech and gained a lot of additional support. A hearing was scheduled a few days later at the capitol in Room 216. The University and College Committee was present and the State Institutions of Higher Learning board was also in attendance. I walked out of my office en route to the meeting and there were people saying, "We're here, Senator, just like you asked us to be." I stopped and shook hands with the supporters. When I walked inside the room where the meeting was being held, I looked around and addressed the chairman of the University and College Committee, asking, "Are you going to hold a meeting?" He didn't respond. I asked a few of the members and they quickly decided not to be a part of it. They didn't even call a meeting to order, so the crowd dispersed for home.

The president of Jackson State University, Dr. Ronald Mason, wanted to discuss his plan with me. When I got back with him I learned that he wanted to discuss a way to merge the universities and colleges. Dr. Mason was trying to work out a solution for merging, which I had no interest in pursuing. My only thought in reference to Dr. Mason was that I didn't realize beforehand that we had a Philistine amongst us. The legislative session closed and we were victorious in avoiding a merger. Supporters were able to get some additional resources for Valley to improve its enrollment and to work more closely with the president to attract more students. In 2011 we were able to put $9.2 million dollars into improving the university in a number of crucial areas. It took this recent kind of rallying to fight off merger and closure of Valley, and I was proud to be a part of it.

In the beginning of 2010, an antibullying bill was passed. The bill required every school district in the state to come up with an antibullying plan. There had been a number of cases across the country where suicide was caused by bullying and Mississippi wanted to avoid such a tragedy. The senate came up with an antibullying law and I was one of the coauthors of the bill. The plan was for a state law to shield students from the harmful effects of teasing. It was known that peer pressure and ridicule of fellow students had sparked some of these unfortunate student incidents. I believe that anytime children make conscious decisions to succumb to pressures by no longer having the desire to live, then the adults must take decisive action to eliminate these potential problems. It is extremely heartbreaking to learn that any child might be harassed while attempting to obtain an education. I feel that when students come to school and become disrespectful to staff members and fellow classmates they should be sent home. If their parents make a decision to show up at the school raising the devil about the suspension, then both of them should do their best to solve the problem. I strongly believe that one can not properly receive an education without the existence of adequate classroom discipline. It simply means that rules and regulations must be in place and followed. I'm hopeful that the next bill that will be passed will address the sagging pants trend among our young males. A few municipalities in various states across the country have considered passing laws banning sagging pants. I would personally like to see that trend ended because young men walking around exposing their underwear this way does nothing to move our people forward; rather it halts our progress.

It was election time for Congressman Bennie Thompson. He was running against an African American Republican, Bill Marcy, formerly of Chicago, Illinois. Marcy was a Republican nominee who came down from Chicago to the Voters' League. When Congressman Thompson was scheduled to speak before the Voters' League, Marcy showed up, unannounced. He wanted an opportunity to challenge the congressman, but I wouldn't allow it and of course that made the headlines of the newspaper. When it was finally said and done, Marcy was not a formidable challenge for Thompson, who had proved himself a competent and well-liked congressman among his constituents. Hence, he was rewarded with another easy but well-deserved victory. I was pleased with my role in helping him to accomplish this.

Besides bearing the stigma of having to contend with numerous racial discrimination suits, Mississippi has an image that has been greatly affected in recent years by a rash of mysterious hangings of black males. Knowing the state's reputation of lynchings and the circumstances surrounding some of these hangings, civil rights leaders have understandably suspected foul play in these deaths, though white state pathologist and law enforcement officials have denied that any racial factors were involved in the fatalities and deemed them mere suicides. According to the *Atlanta Constitution*, there have been nearly sixty hanging deaths in Mississippi since 1987. We are faced with the reality that in the second decade of the twenty-first century we still have black people hanging from trees or other structures and this alone should raise serious questions. The possibility that these hanging deaths were in fact lynchings, however, requires that notable attention be given to finding definitive answers regarding their significant increase.

Hanging by the
Threads of Justice

On December 3, 2010, the body of a twenty-six-year-old African American man by the name of Jermaine Carter was found hanging from an oak tree in a predominately white North Greenwood area of Leflore County. It wasn't long before accounts of this story went all over the country. Jermaine's mother, Brenda Carter, gave me permission to release the pictures of her dead son. I sent the photos of Jermaine hanging from the tree to *The Final Call*, the official newspaper of the sect the Nation of Islam run by Louis Farrakhan. Young Carter's death was ruled by the county coroner a suicide, but there are many who have serious doubts about this assessment, including me.

Jermaine Carter allegedly had some mental challenges. He wandered away from his workplace in Greenwood where he and his stepfather worked together. The stepfather stated that it wasn't unusual for Jermaine to wander off, but he always returned home. It was a Wednesday afternoon when he drifted away and was seen leaving the Highland Park Shopping Center. On Thursday morning there were witnesses who spotted him walking along the streets. It must have been Thursday night when he supposedly hanged himself. The policeman found him on Friday morning just before our Christmas parade. The county sheriff, Ricky Banks, reported that he saw no signs at the scene pointing to it being a murder. However, the scene was never roped off with yellow tape, a normal procedure that I have seen in all crime scenes to keep the area from being contaminated. Banks went on to report that the evidence showed that Jermaine

Carter dragged an old frame of a nearby table, leaned it against the trunk of the tree, and then tied himself to a limb. Banks alleged the frame probably broke because Carter kicked it out from under himself.

Jermaine Carter's family and many community leaders don't believe that it happened the way it was told. People began coming to Greenwood from different parts of the country for the press conferences. I went to visit Brenda Carter the next day after Jermaine's body was discovered. Understandably she was extremely distraught; I showed her the pictures of the crime scene that I was able to obtain. I wanted her to see the condition in which her son had been left, so that she could draw some better conclusions about the matter herself. She looked at me and said, "My son loved life too much to take his own life." I visited the crime scene twice on Saturday, the day following discovery of his body, to view things with my own eyes. I was accompanied by Robert Sims, the vice president of the Voters' League.

There were certainly a lot of unanswered questions, matters that needed more clarification. For example, it was reported that Jermaine had a rope in his pocket, but he didn't have anything to cut it with. Moreover, I felt it was clearly unorthodox procedure not to rope off the crime scene. The tree limb where the hanging took place was nearly twelve feet high; I'm six-two and I couldn't see how I could have maneuvered to hang myself from such an elevated structure. I wanted to know how a boy that was Jermaine's height, considerably shorter than I am, hanged himself from this limb. There were a few people, including myself, who were contacted by *The Final Call* for a statement on this terrible event. I certainly expressed my consternation over the affair and clarified my views about law enforcement findinga more credible explanation of what actually happened. Wendol Lee, who is president of the Memphis-based group Operation Help Civil Rights, looked for real answers and stated, "The area where Jermaine was found hanging is an area that black people do not go into, according to what residents have told us. Blacks get harassed and stopped by the police in that area, so why would this young man go way over there to kill himself? We believe someone took him over there and killed him." Mrs. Valarie Powe, who at the time of *The Final Call* newspaper report was the spokesperson for the family, found relevant questionable issues similar to mine. She stated, "A crime scene was never established. They never roped the scene off and this has not been treated like a crime. There is no reason to believe that he would commit suicide. We appreciate attention being brought to this because we need an outcry from the people."

Carter's death is still a topic of discussion in Greenwood because there are still questions that need answering. The FBI came to Greenwood and launched an immediate investigation but their conclusions also are still pending. The two-year anniversary of the death of Jermaine Carter has passed, a painful reminder of a tragic loss. The theory of the hanging being a suicide remains difficult because his loved ones never accepted this conclusion, so there is no closure for them or the community. His family stated that Jermaine's main problem was that he tended not to defend himself against others in conflict, but they continually maintain that he wouldn't kill himself. It's always a hard adjustment to make when a mother has to bury a child, especially under these kinds of conditions. I was extremely disturbed by this incident and I still feel the same way today as I did when it occurred. My opinion about this matter has never deviated from the first time I visited the crime scene. I feel like we can't have a black man hanging from a tree and go back to business as usual. We as a people just can't sit back and let things of this nature go on. If there is any suspicion that foul play could have been a factor in this case then something must be done to get beyond the suspicion. We can't allow issues like this to get swept under the rug and leave us oblivious to the cruel realities that black people may still be easy victims of vicious racial foul play.

All Infection Is Not Gone

On June 16, 2011, an unknown person fired three shots into my home. It was late Thursday night and Chris and I were in the bed asleep. I thought the noise that I heard had come from somewhere distant until I woke up the next morning. There was a bullet found in the back of my wife's car; another bullet went through a front window and crashed into a wall, and the last bullet ricocheted off the brick exterior. It was a despicable and terrifying act and I hated for my wife to suffer through it. I really can't say for sure what triggered this cowardly act, but a couple of things had occurred that might have been the cause. There were some filmmakers who were at my home to interview me regarding the remake of a 1966 NBC documentary about race in Greenwood. We spent approximately four hours discussing pertinent information that could be useful for the documentary. I don't know if that may have irritated someone who feared not knowing what was being discussed.

I attended a screening of the original documentary later that evening and there were approximately fifty people in attendance. There was an African American male who, after viewing the film, responded that he was "pissed off." I felt that he used a bad choice of words in front of a public audience. His wife and children were also there and I certainly thought he could have been more respectful to them by expressing his displeasure in more appropriate language. The man began to question me concerning why I wasn't part of the membership of the club that was hosting the event. I didn't understand why he was so inquisitive about my status in this particular organization. It was a decent organization that my pastor and many others that I knew were a part of, but this wasn't the setting to inquire about my lack of membership in it. He then went on to say that his anger didn't stem from viewing the film, but was about Greenwood's current conditions. He made a cocky remark claiming that some of the elected officials in the area had automobiles that cost more than a constituent's home. I didn't know what that comment was supposed to mean considering I had bought two new automobiles in the last year. I felt my purchases had nothing to do with the job that I do. I had taught school for many years and I had been quite successful from working extremely hard. I was entitled to buy my wife and myself new vehicles or anything else we could afford because I had earned that right. I find it very disheartening when people want to question the materialistic things that hardworking individuals treat themselves to. I wonder where those same people are when I'm faced with obstacles and difficult tasks in my personal life or while I am working for the welfare of black Mississippians. I was the same man who years ago had gotten a car repossessed, but I kept on going just like I have to do when I'm faced with any other life complication. I didn't know if his comments were general insinuations or if I was the specific individual that he was referring to. It didn't matter either way, however, because my position would remain the same.

This man carried on debating with me to the point that some of the people got up and left. I'm not certain that the meeting had any connection with the shots being fired into my home. It was just peculiar that the assault on my house happened right after the meeting and public awareness of my involvement with the new documentary. I know that I was very shocked when I realized that my property had once again been vandalized.

I called state representative Willie Perkins over to survey the scene with me. Police Chief Henry Purnell arrived on the scene and the Federal Bureau of Investigation and the Mississippi Bureau of Investigation were contacted to assist. I am familiar with a great many of the residents in the Greenwood community since I was born and raised in the area. Hence, I requested a list of all the people who were present at that meeting from the Mississippi Bureau of Investigation, hoping it would provide a lead to the perpetrator. A great deal of time has elapsed since the request and I still haven't received it. I have a serious problem that I haven't been able to secure that list and I haven't heard anything from any law enforcement officials about it. It has been very puzzling that I can't get basic information concerning this case.

Two weeks after this incident, another one, perhaps associated with it, caught my attention. I was leaving my home on my way to a city council meeting. There was a man sitting across the street in a white SUV looking rather suspicious. I kept my eyes on him as I was walking to get into my car and when he noticed me, he began backing his vehicle up. He wouldn't drive past the house, but instead turned and went down a side street. I followed behind him in my vehicle and I was able to obtain his license plate number. I turned the information over to the FBI and the state investigator and it was discovered that he was from Greenwood, though he was residing in Tennessee at that time. He was contacted by law enforcement officials and informed that they wanted to speak with him. His response was that he would be able to accommodate them in a week or so when he was in town. I would have thought it was more urgent to talk with this fellow than law enforcement seemed to be taking it. I just thought the idea of a man parked across from an elected official's home after his house had been the recent target of gunshots would have raised more immediate concerns. I'm very disappointed with the way things continue to unfold with the investigation; it seems as if law enforcement officials are on the job with a mentality of "business as usual." They seem to be saying that the ordeal is already over for Jordan and therefore we can just go on with our everyday routine. I understand better than anyone about being able to move on to the next task, but something has to happen. I have been the target of malicious behavior on too many occasions already. It has only been by the grace of God that I or my family members have not suffered serious physical tragedy as victims of these senseless acts of violence. I don't know if these acts are thought of as scare tactics or if someone is truly hoping to cause harm to me or one of my family members, but the reason doesn't matter because nothing can justify them and they are definitely unlawful. Each time I get comfortable in healing wounds from the past something else happens to remind me that the infection of racial hatred is not all the way gone.

In the summer of 2011, my last brother, Will Henry, made his transition from this life. He had fought a long arduous battle, but on July 28, 2011, God called him home. It is always a difficult thing to say goodbye to any of your loved ones, but I realize through my own journey that it is a part of life. It is Sister and I that are left among the siblings to keep close tabs on one another and we will always continue to do just that. The rest of my immediate family members are doing well. Chris and I have great-grandchildren now to add to the Jordan clan. I feel good knowing that we have laid a solid foundation for our future generations to follow. We have set examples that hard work and dedication will always pay off.

On September 24, 2011, the town of Glendora, Mississippi, held a grand reopening of the Emmett Till Historic Intrepid Center. The center was originally opened in 2005. The Till Center is located on the grounds of the old Glendora cotton gin. Glendora is the town where Till was brutally beaten. The event drew people from Mississippi and other states as well. The mayor, Johnny B. Thomas, felt that it was only right that the healing should begin in the place where the premeditation started. He stated, "Today, on behalf of the citizens of Glendora, we want to welcome you to help us initiate the healing." Development specialist Temita S. Davis was in charge of the project, which included interior upgrades and full renovations to the structure. She was the program guide for the grand reopening. Mrs. Davis, the mayor, and the development team were all dressed in black and white, symbolic of blacks and whites coming together; an orange ribbon adorned the building to represent the healing process. It was an excellent gesture of unity and I believe the program was quite significant.

I was one of several speakers invited to address the crowd. I wanted people to understand that I truly applauded the efforts to bring healing. I said, "Healing does not take place unless all the infection is moved out of the sore." I pointed out that in this year, 2011, my house had been shot into and a black man, James Anderson, was deliberately run over and killed in Jackson, only because he was black. Four white teens pled guilty to a hate crime. Daryl Dedmon was given a life sentence. These things did not happen in 1955; they happened in 2011. I reflected on the Emmett Till murder and still deemed it to be the worst in the history of this country. I told the gathering it was left up to us to see that justice prevailed. I realize that we have made tremendous progress as a people, but we must not close our eyes to concerns that need immediate attention. The shooting at my home, the death of an innocent African American man in a terrible hate crime, and the mysterious hanging of a black young man with his whole future ahead of him are issues that need investigating. If we want to be completely healed, I said, then we must continue to move forward and not be afraid to seek answers to any and all acts perpetrated against us inspired by racial hatred.

The Journey Continues . . .

A t the end of the summer of 2011, I was working a very busy schedule because there were a lot of hearings taking place concerning funding for Head Start programs. There are many groups and individuals who feel that money intended for Head Start is not filtering down properly and I'm hearing their concerns on this matter. I am awaiting the report from the Mississippi Department of Human Services on their findings concerning the subject. The people who have registered the complaint against the Planning Development District will be present and they will also be reporting to an upcoming senate committee hearing. There are problems in the Mississippi Development Authority that need addressing. My responsibility as chairman of the Investigative State Offices Committee is to get involved in all these kinds of issues and help to resolve them.

The Greenwood city council is moving along pretty smoothly and we're working closely with Valley State University. The city of Greenwood is attempting to charge Valley State University thirty thousand dollars a year for fire protection. The city council maintains that this is entirely too costly. Our position is that if there is a fire on campus, Valley should be charged at that time rather than such an enormous sum annually. The city council received the public school budget and we are mandated by state law to approve it. A few of the council members requested that the superintendent, Dr. Margie Pulley, come to the Greenwood City Council and personally explain where and how the money is going to be spent. She isn't required to comply, so she did not oblige that request. Her position was that if anyone wanted to know about the school budget then they should attend a school board meeting or check specifically with her office. I agreed totally with her decision because the budget is already explained as it is established. There was no millage change in the budget and the people who were demanding that she visit the city council don't even have children in the public school system. The superintendent is doing a great job and I applaud her success.

The council has been able to strengthen the curfew law to keep our youngsters off the streets. The law mandates that all children be in their homes by 10:00 p.m. on school nights. We also cracked down on cars playing loud music as they travel the streets. There have been incidents when the vibrations from the speakers in these cars were so strong that they shook the pictures on the walls of the homes situated along the streets. Previously there was a one-hundred-dollar fine for offenders, but it was increased to a thousand-dollar fine and the vehicle can be impounded on the second or third offense. I'm happy to say that this law has made Greenwood relatively quiet.

The state of Mississippi is celebrating the first ever African American of any major political party as a nominee for governor. Democrat Johnny Dupree, the nominee, is no stranger to politics and he definitely has a good track record to prove it. He's served on the Hattiesburg Public School Board and in 2001 he became the first African American mayor of Hattiesburg, the state's third-largest city. He was reelected twice during the past decade. He has been successful during his tenure as mayor in Hattiesburg. He started his success by decreasing the crime rate and he brought over a thousand new jobs into the city. He balanced the budget quite well, a particularly noteworthy achievement in this day's climate of weak economies almost everywhere. President Obama received the support that put him in office in the 2012 election. He has my vote, as he did when he won the party primary. Dupree's candidacy is significant for all of us. Indicative of the possibilities for even a state like Mississippi with an ugly past of racial oppression, Dupree's candidacy, win or lose, is the type of history that students will be reading about for a long time and coincides with the unique historical event that President Barack Obama's victory meant for Americans of all racial groups.

My advice to the young generation is they must learn to burn the midnight oil in order to obtain a good education. In the process of seeking an education, they must learn to give God some of their time. It's extremely important for younger generations to stay focused on the goals they want to accomplish. It is essential to seek a good education because one will find it almost impossible to succeed in life without it. It's time to end the senseless distractions that young people make a part of their everyday routine. The television, cell phones, and music can become major distractions if our youth are not careful. It is left up to us as parents to monitor our children's devotion to these types of activities. I see a lot of students majoring in criminal justice here in Mississippi and acquiring degrees in the discipline, but they can't find a job or won't make a decent salary if they do. Most of them are unable to teach in the classrooms so they end up finding work in some form of law enforcement. A starting salary for a teacher in the state of Mississippi is thirty-one thousand dollars and a criminal justice job starts at eighteen thousand dollars. I want students to not always look for what is easy, but to consider what is needed for our people to advance. Knowledge can't be reduced to something that is poured into someone's head; students are going to have to sweat to reach certain education goals. We have to be responsible for teaching our children and making sure they know their history. We tend to take our history the way it is given to us by other people. When children look around and don't see any African Americans in responsible positions, they assume that is acceptable. Those of us who have come through the ranks of life and have accomplished some things of substance know about sacrifices. In some instances, it may take one many years of work and sacrifice to actually see real success in life. If two persons are a young married couple like my wife and I were when we embarked on our life of work, and soon thereafter start a family, it might take even longer to reach some goals, but you still keep working at it. You never give up and you work closely together to maintain the family unit. It saddens me today to see how the family structure has been almost destroyed.

Moreover, we have drifted away from basic principles as a people. We don't care about one another as we should and I don't want the younger generation to ever think that this is acceptable behavior. I fault integration as a part of the reason for us drifting apart as a people. Our integration into society is something we marched, begged, and fought for, but it's not and was never considered the complete answer to where the race needs to be headed. It certainly appears to have been the case that when we were going through difficult times we were closer to each other. Some of us feel that we have overcome, that everything among the races is equal, but this illusion has adversely affected us in so many ways. We clearly have other rivers to cross, rivers fraught with racism, poverty, crime, and hopelessness. It is a tragic reality but America is not yet free of its past and all the turmoil surrounding us validates that conclusion.

My views on what injures the black community are varied and perhaps even controversial. But in my lifetime I've seen much that could have been done to shape our development as a real force in this nation and how these factors have been neglected, ignored, or by design simply thwarted by people who have no real interest in black advancement. When one looks at what the Republicans are doing in Washington against an African American president it is easy to understand exactly how they feel about the rest of us, the average black person. If they're against President Obama and will not cooperate with him in his efforts to address the nation's problems, then it shows us what we are really up against. They are determined to do anything to insure his failure and it has as much to do with the color of his skin as it does about his politics or policies. Their thinking is just as much an example of how they feel about blacks in general.

We must learn to control our own communities, especially economically, and not depend on outsiders. We are not spending our resources wisely; maybe instead of drinking eight or nine quarts of beer weekly, it should be cut down to one. The remainder of the money could be saved and perhaps used toward something more beneficial. We also need to get stronger leadership in some of our churches. We accept the inevitability of dying, but God wants us to live a righteous life so we will have somewhere to go when our time is up here on earth. It's important to live a good life so one is a legacy to someone coming along behind him. I hope the hard times that we are enduring now can get us where we need to be as a people. There are some who believe that being born black means you're less than someone else and that you have to be submissive to whites in order to make it in life without serious struggle. It doesn't mean that at all, but if we want a place in the sun then we have to be qualified to obtain it. A person can't skin and grin and be credible to his people. A person must be proficient at what he or she does and must demand respect as a member of the human race. A person should always have the courage to stand up for what is right and treat his own kind with dignity and respect.

Well, it's time for me to hit the campaign trail. I have my car loaded with campaign materials and I have my two workers accompanying me. We're going to visit Tallahatchie, Holmes, and Leflore counties. I look forward to meeting and greeting the people because I am usually welcomed with such a warm reception. They tell me how much I am appreciated and they have certainly proved it. I have never lost a race where African Americans were key voters and that makes me feel wonderful. My mission is to continue to get the job done and make life better for others. If this book encourages just one person not to allow ignorance, prejudice, and hatred to write their epitaph, then I have done my job!

Epilogue

I t's a cool breezy morning in the state of Mississippi. I'm up bright
and early preparing for election day. It's November 8, 2011, and
today will determine if I serve another term as state senator or
if my tenure in state office has come to an end. My wife, Chris, has
been through this day with me numerous times before and I still receive the same support from her that I received when I won my first
political seat. The campaigning for another opportunity to serve the
people would be determined today. My son Don took time to drive
over from Texas to chauffeur me around to the precincts. It was such
an amazing feeling because everywhere we stop I receive a warm
welcome. There are young and old people informing me that I had
received their vote and that was quite an uplifting feeling. The idea
of the people from Mississippi having that much faith and confidence in me has always meant a lot to me.

I went from stop to stop embracing my supporters to let them
know how greatly I appreciated them and their support. I received
the final results from the election that night via television. I won with
over 81.5 percent of the vote. I actually didn't encounter the problems
that I anticipated from my opponent, Rogrick Wardell. Chris and I
were extremely happy to know that I had won another term in state
office. It was a disappointment that Johnny Dupree wasn't able to
get into office, but I'm confident that we haven't seen the last of him.
He set a precedent after he won the primary election and that itself
was a victory. We had never had an African American win a primary
for a gubernatorial election and this was a major accomplishment.
I believe that if he runs again he will be successful. The Republicans

have gained control of the senate and the house, but we'll continue to work together toward what is best for the people.

The voter ID bill passed, which most black Democratic leaders opposed, but it still remains a battle at another level that we'll have to wage. There was another major goal that we reached in Greenwood and that was electing our first African American circuit clerk. I have been in politics for the past forty-six years and we have always encountered trouble with this particular office. This is the office where people register to vote. This time a young friend of mine with a bright future ahead of him won that office. His name is Elmus Stockstill and he won off a ballot from the Voters' League. He was formerly in charge of the congressman's office in Greenwood and now he's the circuit clerk in Leflore County. It's a great accomplishment to have an African American in that position because it is arguably the most important office in the county. After the absentee ballots were counted, Annie Conley, a black woman, was declared winner of the seat as the tax collector's office. I just feel great about the whole process because African Americans had the greatest turnout in over three decades. The fact that Johnny Dupree ran for governor certainly triggered a massive turnout of African Americans. I was quite pleased to see that kind of progress being made. I want African Americans to continue to move forward in taking advantage of the opportunities that become available. Clearly much in Mississippi and in Greenwood needs to be done, though black people have also accomplished much and continue to advance. I can promise that David Jordan will remain on the battlefield committed to making a difference!

Index